MEANING IN LIFE AS EXPERIENCED BY PERSONS LABELED RETARDED IN A GROUP HOME

MEANING IN LIFE AS EXPERIENCED BY PERSONS LABELED RETARDED IN A GROUP HOME

A Participant Observation Study

By

Lous Heshusius, Ph.D.

Department of Teaching and Department of Special Education
University of Northern Iowa
Cedar Falls, Iowa

CHARLES C THOMAS · PUBLISHER
Springfield · Illinois · U.S.A.

Published and Distributed Throughout the World by
BANNERSTONE HOUSE
301-327 East Lawrence Avenue, Springfield, Illinois, U.S.A.

ISBN 0-398-04064-8 (cloth)
0-398-04079-6 (paper)
Library of Congress Catalog Card Number: 80-15181

Printed in the United States of America
N-11

Library of Congress Cataloging in Publication Data

Heshusius, Lous.
Meaning in life as experienced by persons labeled retarded in a group home.

Bibliography: p.
Includes index.
1. Mentally handicapped—Case studies. I. Title.
HV3004.H46 362.3'092'6 80-15181
ISBN 0-398-04064-8
ISBN 0-398-04079-6 (pbk.)

PREFACE

DURING MY YEARS as a graduate student in special education, one aspect of the coursework and the literature my fellow students and I were exposed to became increasingly bothersome to me, to the point of becoming intolerable. This was the virtual absence of the voices of the people most involved — the exceptional persons themselves.

While examining theories, positions, and research findings that reflected what *we,* the professionals, thought should be done and how we should do it, *they,* the persons we had labeled this way or that, were rarely asked what they thought about their own matters. While I felt sure that the Special Education profession at large was truly concerned about the quality of life and welfare of those it had taken under its care, I was equally sure that something of importance was missing—the self-perception of the individuals within the client groups we attempted to serve.

If we are sincere in our concern about quality of life for the persons in our care (a concern that has in recent years been expressed in the literature as one greatly in need of attention, and one which is inherent in the principles of normalization and in the mandate of the least restrictive alternative) then we must foremost recognize that a judgment of life's quality must be made whenever possible by the person who does the living.

Having lived and worked in several different cultures, it has become evident to me that definitions of quality of life vary greatly among cultures and among subgroups. Radically different quality indices exist not only across cultures but also across groups and individuals. The lesson of this experience has been that no one has the right *nor* the knowledge to define quality in living for another. To whatever extent possible we must inform ourselves of the unique perspective held by persons who need our assistance within their own social/phenomenological reality.

Dominant analytic paradigms of correlational and experimental research have not been helpful gathering such information. Theories of mental retardation have typically been generated from sources other than the social/cultural reality. In addition, stereotypes held by lay and professional persons alike have cast the less competent as unable to reflect upon and evaluate their lives.

However, the horizon of research paradigms in the social sciences is widening. Studies employing qualitative and naturalistic modes of inquiry are increasingly complementing the literature with data that focus on qualitative understanding and on meaning.

This book reports the results of an investigation that asked the question how persons who lived in a group home for the retarded experienced meaning or lack of meaning, in their day-to-day lives. To that end, the naturalistic research strategy of participant observation was employed. In presenting the results I have preserved the basic structure of the research process by which they emerged, both with regard to data gathering and data analysis. Too often, reports of qualitative research have been criticized for leaving the reader uninformed of how and from how many data the findings were generated. By reflecting the research processes in the presentation of this study, the reader will have the empirical base to form her/his own judgment of credibility and significance.

The behavioral patterns that emerged from the data, and around which the chapters are organized, deal with the subjects' views on (1) independence, (2) marriage and related issues (subjects' views on the possibility and values of marriage, physical/sexual involvement, having children, and boy/girlfriend relationships), (3) understanding and manipulation of interpersonal behavior, and (4) intrapersonal understanding (subjects' views on their status as a mental retardate, their competency, and lack of competency).

That profound implications for program planning and further research exist, if we decide to start listening to the persons we label incompetent, is evident from the results of this study and from findings by the very few naturalistic studies of similar focus. These data show that there are major discrepancies between what we decide for the persons we designate retarded and what they want for themselves. This is especially the case as it relates to the possibility of marriage, sexual expression, relationships, and the degree of independence allowed. What they ask for is not something that would do anyone else, or themselves, any harm. Therefore, the ultimate question the results of this study pose goes back to ourselves: Why do we more often than not stand in the way of these persons' search for more meaningful living?

L.H.

ACKNOWLEDGMENTS

FOR THEIR THOUGHTFUL comments on the various drafts of the manuscript, I extend my gratitude to the following persons: Dr. Samuel Guskin and Dean William Lynch of Indiana University, Dr. Melvyn Semmel of the University of California at Santa Barbara, and Dean Burton Blatt and Dr. Robert Bogdan of Syracuse University. I am particularly appreciative to Dr. William Corsaro of Indiana University for his advice and methodological assistance during the conduct of the research that led to this book and for his valuable reactions to the research report. For their fine editorial assistance, I would like to thank Lane Toler and Art Bedard.

For their cooperation and for their receptivity to the aim of the study, I thank the staff of the group home where the research was conducted: Mrs. M. Burton, Director; Mr. Dave Barber, Coordinator; and the houseparents, Steve Hettlinger, Mat Leffers, Elaine Strain, and Tim Terrell.

To the subjects of the study, my deepest gratitude is due. Their straightforwardness and their unique personalities provided a rich source for observation and understanding of behavior, including, and I believe particularly so, an understanding of ways in which we construe our own reality. I hope this study may help us to become partners of the persons we label retarded in their search for a more meaningful life to a greater extent than we have.

L.H.

CONTENTS

MEANING IN LIFE AS EXPERIENCED BY PERSONS LABELED RETARDED IN A GROUP HOME

Chapter 1

PURPOSE AND BACKGROUND OF THE STUDY

THE CONCERN OF THIS study was to examine some of the ways in which young adults, labeled retarded, experienced meaning in day-to-day living. The subjects were five women and three men who lived in a group home and worked in a sheltered workshop.

The study searched to isolate behavioral patterns that were valid for most of these persons most of the time. Data were gathered during eight months of extensive participant observation, a research methodology that draws data from daily happenings, that is, from what subjects do, say, and react to as they go about living their lives.

The central question addressed by this study was: What are important realities in the lives of these persons? Concretely, this concern yielded questions for focusing investigation, such as: What particular aspects of life concern them? What occupies their thinking? What do they talk about, dream about, laugh, cry, and worry about? Do they try to manipulate, or try to escape? What elicits their reaction, anger, or pleasure? What do they do? What do they like and dislike? What do they think about their living and working situations? In sum, how do they make sense of their lives?

The need for phenomenologically oriented knowledge

In 1967, Edgerton noted that the literature failed to provide us with an appreciation of what the lives of persons designated retarded are like. No existing report dealt at all adequately with the details of their everyday lives or with their own reactions to themselves and their lives.

With the exception of some recent studies, knowledge of how persons labeled retarded make sense out of their lives continues to be conspicuously absent from the professional literature. Their own thoughts, emotions, and evaluations of their lives have rarely been documented. "The defectives, not expected to think, were never asked to comment on the matter," Blatt (1977, p. 8) pointedly states.

The conviction that knowledge of this kind is critical if we are to assist the less competent in our care to live meaningful lives emerges from a phenomenological orientation. It essentially reflects the dictum by W. I. Thomas: "If men define situations as real, they are real in their consequences." Taylor and Bogdan (1977) express the phenomenological orientation with regard to the less competent when they state that for the phenomenologist and the qualitative researcher alike, there is no truth or reality; reality differs from person to person, from staff to resident, from administrator to ward attendant.

Why would one want to find out about these multiple realities and, in this case, about the reality as lived by persons labeled retarded? Such knowledge does not render rules, techniques, and steps for modifying and structuring behavior. The latter outcomes are the results of the most prominent empirical-analytic paradigm of inquiry. The practicality of phenomenological ways of knowing lies in understanding, as originally expressed in the German word "Verstehen," which may be translated as "partaking the common meaning." Partaking in common meaning is extremely practical. It increases deliberateness and reflectivity and can lead to clearer communication.* Moreover, it provides the profession with a set of guidelines to assist the less competent in our care to live their lives in a way most meaningful to them.

The few naturalistic studies that have investigated how persons labeled retarded make sense of their lives have found that these persons live according to their own perceptions of what is meaningful, regardless of what we, the mental retardation profes-

*For an elaborate discussion on the different practical uses of knowledge rendered by different paradigms of inquiry, see Van Manen, M. Linking ways of knowing with ways of being practical. *Curriculum Inquiry,* 1977, 6, 205-229.

sionals, tell them they should value. These studies used qualitative data-gathering procedures of participant observation and/ or interviewing. The studies focused on their subjects' perceptions of themselves and their lives. Edgerton (1967) investigated the lives of forty-eight persons who had been discharged from a state hospital after an average stay of two years. They had lived in the community as free citizens without any formal supervision for an average of six years. Research procedures consisted of participant observation and interviewing. The mean number of contact hours for each respondent was seventeen.

Edgerton and Bercovici (1976) conducted a follow-up study of thirty of the subjects of the Edgerton's (1967) study twelve to fourteen years later, to determine what effect the passage of time had had on their community adjustment as evaluated by the subjects as well as by the researchers. No details concerning the extent of participant observation were noted, nor the number of contact hours.

In another study, Henshel (1972) interviewed fifty Anglo and Chicano persons (and their spouses) who had been labeled retarded by various agencies but had never been institutionalized. The research utilized semistructured interviews, carried out as informal dialogues. Three visits were arranged to each of the subjects over a ten-month period.

Bogdan and Taylor (1976) provide us with an insider's view of mental retardation, an account of what it is like to be assigned the status of a mental retardate. The account was obtained through an intensive unstructured interview project, which resulted in an autobiography.

The major findings of the studies here noted will be discussed in their relation to the data of the present study, in Chapters 3 through 7.

The need for ecologically valid data

The professional literature has been criticized for yielding knowledge that lacks meaning for real-life situations. The greatest part of research in the area of mental retardation has been obtained by experimental and correlational paradigms, which isolate and correlate variables by manipulating the environment, thus creating a laboratory situation. Not often have researchers gone where the persons labeled retarded live their regular lives to study their behavior, the setting, and the interaction. Findings, consequently, lack ecological validity, however interesting they may be in relation to isolated psychological and learning concepts.

The present study is grounded in an ecological perspective, which, with regard to mental retardation, has been expressed by Brooks and Baumeister (1977, p. 412) as follows:

> Apparently there is a real phenomenon, which is called mental retardation, that can be identified by the layman (usually with less elegant names) and that will exist independently of the culture's attempts to formalize the concept. Indeed, that which society views as retarded behavior *is* the first and only "true" criterion for defining retarded behavior; without those naive judgements, there would be no phenomenon and nothing to measure.

As these authors state, it is only where those persons live that adaptive behavior can be analyzed into components that perhaps then can become a basis for development of dependent measures. By extension, it is only there that their behavior can give us some indication how they see life as meaningful or not meaningful.

SETTING

The subjects in this study lived in a group home and worked in a sheltered workshop. The workshop and the group home were within 400 yards of each other, and both were administered by the local Council for Retarded Citizens.

The group home consisted of two houses (one for the men, one for the women), commonly referred to as "the cottages." These cottages were rented from a university training center. Thus, the cottages were part of a larger group of buildings, which were located at the edge of a midwestern university campus. These buildings were separated from the rest of the campus by a highway and were within walking distance of two shopping centers and of residential areas.

At the time of the research the two cottages housed respectively five men between the ages of nineteen and thirty and a cottage parent (single male) and five women between the ages of seventeen and thirty-eight and cottage parents (a couple). The layout of these two cottages is identical. Figures 1 and 2 (first and second floor, respectively) show the facilities of the cottages. The cottage parent (s) occupied the living room and bedroom of the first floor (Figure 1) as private quarters. The second floor provided bedrooms for the subjects.

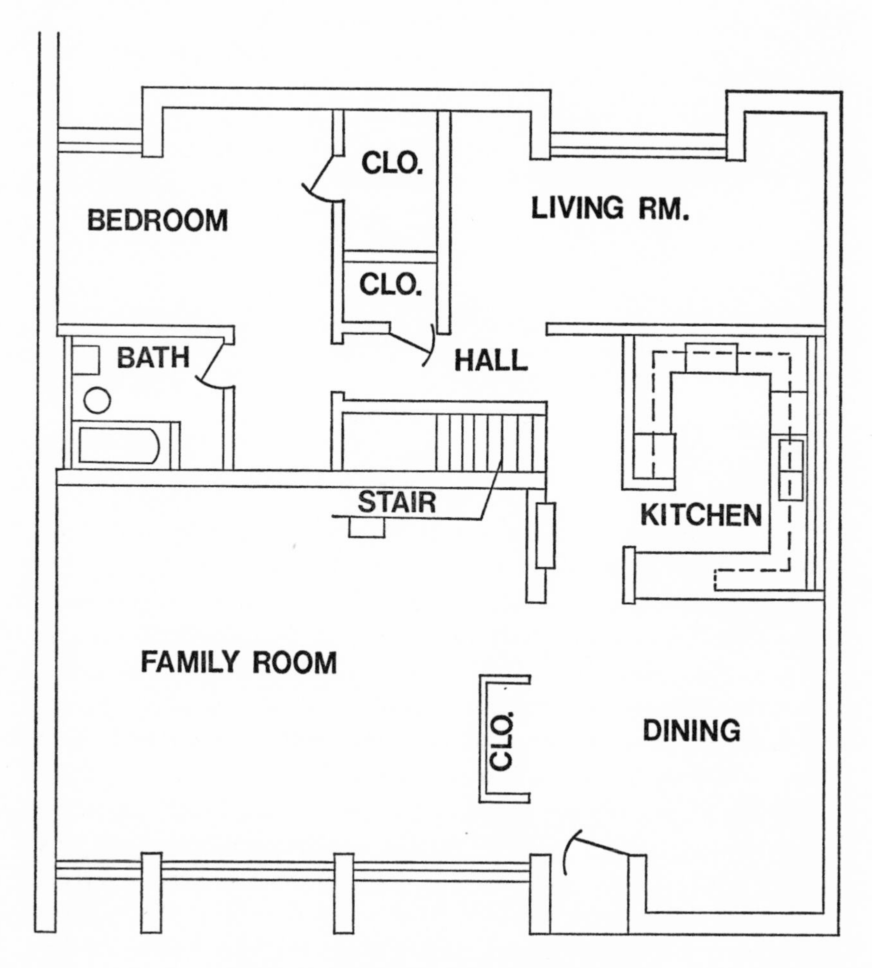

Figure 1. First floor of group home site.

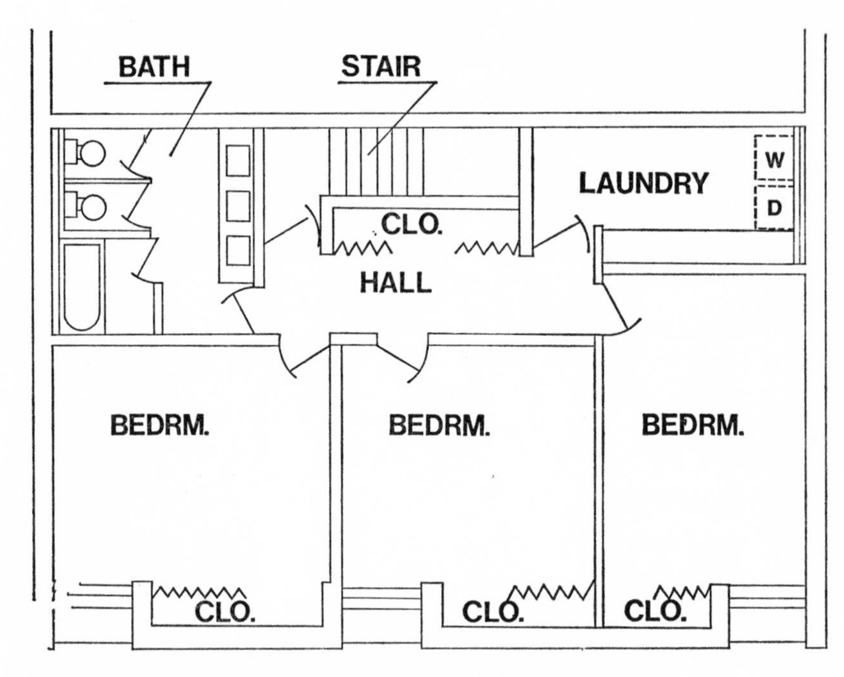

Figure 2. Second floor of group home site.

SUBJECTS

The purpose of the study was not to render case studies or clinical interpretations but, rather, to find patterns of ongoing behavior in real-life settings that were typical for most subjects most of the time. Therefore, only a minimum of personal information on the subjects was obtained at the start of the research; I believed that without such information I would be less biased in obtaining and reporting subjects' perceptions of themselves and their lives. Table I shows the initial information.

Of the eight subjects, five (Terry, Kitty, Pam, Lisa, and Rob) had verbal skills that allowed regular interaction; three subjects (Jane, Don and Max) showed speech problems that made conversation somewhat more difficult, but not impossible. Two other nonsubjects lived in the male cottage during the period of research. These persons (Bob and Tim) lacked verbal skills to the extent that regular verbal interaction was not possible. How-

Table I

Sex, Age, and Diagnoses of the Subjects

*Names**	*Sex*	*Age*	*Diagnoses*
Terry	F	17	emotional problems — slight organic defect
Kitty	F	24	cerebral palsy
Pam	F	18	epilepsy
Lisa	F	38	Down's syndrome
Jane	F	26	epilepsy
Rob	M	19	RH factor
Don	M	29	mental retardation, cause obscure
Max	M	23	mentally ill — mentally retarded

*All names are fictitious.

ever, they took part in all events and contributed to the data indirectly because of their interactions with the subjects.

After all data were collected, the subjects' personal files were examined and short descriptions were written of each person, indicating family background, school experiences, diagnostic information, and test scores. These descriptons can be found in Appendix A. The reader has the choice to approach the remainder of this report with or without this information.

All subjects worked in the sheltered workshop from 8 A.M. till 4 P.M. daily. Kitty and Don worked in the workshop's recycling plant and all other subjects worked in vocational training programs.

From 4 P.M. till bedtime (around 10 P.M.) the subjects would spend their time at the group home. After work they did their chores (cleaning house, doing their laundry, and helping with food preparation) or they talked and watched television. After supper the television was the main focus of entertainment. Structured recreational activities took place two or three times a week. On weekends, there would be outings into the community or social activities in the cottages. From the many examples in Chapters 3 through 6 the reader will obtain a more detailed picture of the setting and the ways in which the subjects spent their time.

Chapter 2

METHODOLOGY

A STUDY THAT ATTEMPTS to render ecological valid data without resorting to control over variables classifies as a naturalistic study. While the literature reflects various definitions of the naturalistic paradigm of inquiry, their differences are often a matter of emphasis or scope. The common denominator of most definitions refers to what the researcher does: events are to stay to the greatest possible degree unarranged by the investigator.*

That a pure naturalistic investigation is not possible by known research methods has been discussed, among others, by Edgerton (1975) and Willems (1969). Edgerton (1975) states that no existing methodology for the study of human behavior adequately satisfies the principles of naturalism, which he cites to be (1) that phenomena be seen in their relevant context, (2) that these phenomena be seen not only through the observer's eyes, but those of the subjects as well, and (3) that reactive procedures be avoided at the same time that the investigator regards himself as a part of the phenomena under investigation.

Naturalistic research strategies minimize the influence that the conduct of the research may have on the phenomena of interest. These strategies are conceptually described in the literature. However, the investigator's immersion in a unique and fluctuating real-life setting necessitates that these research strategies are adapted to the characteristics of each setting and that the particular adaptations play a role in the nature and the validity of

*For an elaborate discussion of naturalistic paradigms of inquiry see e.g. Willems, E. P. and Raush, H. L. (Eds.) *Naturalistic Viewpoints in Psychological Research.* New York: Holt, Rinehart, and Winston, 1969.

the findings that will emerge from them. Hence, it is important to account for the details of all data collection, coding, and analysis procedures.

In the present study the procedures for data collection can be broken down into the the following: entering the field and participant observation, taking field notes, and presentation of self. These procedures will be outlined below. A more detailed and complete account can be read in the original research report (Heshusius, 1978).

DATA COLLECTION

Entering the Field and Participant Observation

Participant observation is variously called participant observation, field observation, qualitative observation, or direct observation. Becker and Geer (1970) define participant observation as a method in which the observer participates in the daily lives of the persons under study over some length of time, observing things that happen and listening to what is said to see what kinds of situations people ordinarily meet and how they behave in them. The researcher enters into conversation with some or all subjects during these situations and discovers their interpretations of the events s/he observed.

Participant observation is not an esoteric strategy. Every day, people in all walks of life carry on this kind of interweaving of looking, listening, and asking. The researcher differs in that s/he does so with self-consciousness and intended awareness (Lofland, 1971).

What and where

In May 1977, an exploratory visit was made to the sheltered workshop. This visit was a regular "tour" offered for interested persons. A similar visit was arranged to the residential facilities. These tours did not provide the opportunity to interact with potential subjects. Such an opportunity came when one of the houseparents, to whom I expressed an interest in closer interaction with the residents, extended an invitation for dinner. The residents appeared to function at a level that could render sufficient qualitative and quantitative data. Permission to conduct the study was subsequently obtained.

The first few weeks, participant observation took place during the structured recreation periods, known to the subjects as "social club." Later, visits to their work and to the residential cottages were added, as well as joining in community outings. Soon, visits to the workshop diminished since observations rendered few data as work rules were rather strict and prohibited interaction with the subjects, nor was there much interaction among the subjects or with their supervisors. However, I continued to pay an occasional visit to the workshop in order to maintain contact with their working life.

Visits to the residential cottages were made on week days and weekends, during the day and in the evenings. Besides these visits to the cottages, there were many outside events to attend. We went out for refreshments or dinner, on shopping trips, bowling, horseback riding, swimming, and rollerskating. We went for a hayride, to a ballgame, to church, to the library, to concerts, and to a circus performance. I also attended parties at the cottages, and on a few occasions the subjects visited my home. During the structured recreational activities, I participated in arts and crafts, ballgames, exercises, and singing. There was only one activity that was somewhat prearranged for the sake of this study. Pam, one of the subjects, had mentioned that she liked religious and "serious" music, so I invited her to a concert. When another subject heard about this, she, too, wanted to go. The first visit to my house was also arranged in reaction to a subject's comment, as shown in the following excerpt from the field notes: Jane asked where I lived. She then said: "Have I been to your house? When I replied that she had not, she said: "You should invite Lisa, Terry, Pam, and Kitty and me to your house and have a party. . ." I told her I thought that was a good idea and would do so one day. (September 13, visit 49)

During the second half of the research, I used opportunities to be alone with the subjects. This was done in order to have a chance for a more intensive interaction, which would allow me to channel the conversation into a desired direction and to obtain information of a more personal nature.

In addition to the participant observation periods, weekly staff meetings were regularly attended. These meetings provided information about ongoing events as well as complimentary information on the subjects.

How much?

Participant observation was continuous in that regular contact with the setting and subjects was maintained over an eight-month period. In all, the study involved over 200 hours of participant observation spread over ninety visits. In addition, many social visits were made during which no data was gathered.

Observation periods were typically two to three hours, though one hour visits and visits of five or more hours also occurred. It is of interest to note that two to three hour visits rendered as much data as the five to seven hour periods. Taylor and Bogdan (1977) suggest that a participant observer should seldom spend more than an hour at a time in the field, especially in the beginning. This is about the maximum amount of time one can record in one's memory everything that goes on. Thus, the one hour delineation has to do with the amount of data one can record. However, being in the field as a participant/observer necessitated on many occasions being there for longer amounts of time due to the very nature of the events in which I was participating. Taylor and Bogdan (1977) appear to delineate the role of the researcher as an observer/participant rather than participant/observer (a distinction made by Lofland, 1971). In this study I clearly took the role as participant/observer. This often meant spending two to six hours in the field to watch ballgames, attend church, or watch movies. These longer stays contributed to establishing rapport and a sense of continuity, and, therefore, to the process of becoming a part of the setting, which would enhance the validity of the data.

Asking questions

During the initial data collection (a four-month period) questions posed to the subjects were mainly reactive to what they said or did. The entire focus was on letting the subjects and their lives speak without intrusion or direction. The field notes show that I used a lot of phrases like "I see . . ." or "Hm, that is interesting." Often I would repeat a key phrase the subject had said and would add ". . . that is what you think?" or simply not respond verbally, which often would encourage continuation. During the second part of the research the questions became more active and conversations were channeled into a direction I desired. This was in line with the approach used for data collection, coding, and analysis to which this discussion will turn shortly. The examples of the field notes in Chapters 3 through 6 will show this gradual intensification in the questions asked.

Becoming part of the setting appeared to happen smoothly and quickly. A striking fact was the friendliness and willingness to interact on the part of the subjects. Except for Pam and Dave, who kept distant for several weeks, they seemed pleased to interact and, even more so, seemed to appreciate having the chance to talk seriously about issues that concerned them. Edgerton (1967), whose subjects reacted similarly to the researcher's presence, states that acceptance and friendliness possibly indicated the loneliness of many of these people and their eagerness to attach themselves to anyone who would listen politely to their life stories and problems. In the present study the latter reason may also pertain. Also, my continuous and absolute denial of authority (to be discussed shortly) may have taken away any potential threat.

It was also made clear to the subjects that I could not do anything for them, e.g. helping them get an apartment or solving interpersonal conflicts. It was stressed that I was there only to be with them, talk with them, and learn from them. In the light of existing stereotypes of mental retardation, it was striking that the subjects welcomed (some of them eagerly) someone to talk with seriously about themselves and their lives while not receiving any tangible benefits in return. Lisa expressed this quite concisely in the following excerpt:

> Lisa and I had coffee after having been to the bank. We had had quite a conversation for about an hour about her feelings on living in the cottage, her idea of a home, and her status as a mental retardate. I asked her if people

talked with her about all these things. She answered: "No." When I asked if she liked talking like that, she replied: "Oh, yes, it is good . . . letting your hair down . . . you know what I mean . . . getting it off your chest," and she added, "but they never have time for you . . . to sit down and try to understand you, you know." (January 21, visit 84)

Field Notes

A most essential feature of participant observation is the writing of field notes. Field notes *are* the actual observations from which the behavioral patterns emerge during data analysis.

During the initial data collection phase, field notes constituted a chronological account, as accurate as possible, of everything I could remember: descriptions of settings, behaviors, and events.

To increase accuracy and completeness of field notes and to claim some statements as verbatim, numerous notes were jotted down while in the field in a small notebook. These notes consisted of key words indicating specific incidents, their nature or sequence, and verbatim phrases jotted down within five to ten minutes after they occurred. These notes were made in private places: toilets appeared particularly handy for such activity, as well as the staff quarters to which I had access while the subjects did not. Notes were never taken in the subjects' presence.

Three conventions are used in reporting conversations: (1) verbatim phrases are quoted between quotation marks as usual, (2) phrases that had not been jotted down while in the field, but which I remembered well, are quoted without quotation marks, and (3) conversations or part of conversations not remembered verbatim are written out in a narrative manner, e.g. "He said that . . . ."

Typically, these notes were immediately outlined upon coming home, which was five minutes after finishing participant observation, and worked out into full field notes. Since the field notes *are* the observations from which the behavioral patterns emerged, the reader will know what the field notes are like by reading the examples in later chapters. These illustrations are segments of the field notes, except for some necessary editing: (1) all names of all persons and institutions are changed, (2) the setting is often summarized in one or two sentences, and (3) the grammatical structure of the sentences has been corrected where necessary.

Presentation of Self

In discussing the judgment of credibility of a qualitative study, Glaser and Strauss (1968) include as an influencing factor how the researcher might have appeared to the various people whom s/he studied. These authors also note that development of trust is critical; otherwise, the analysis suffers. How is trust to be developed? Can there be too much trust? Is one to become a friend or remain a stranger? Is one to be honest or to stay as vague as possible? Does one give opinions when asked, or take sides? These questions center around human relation skills employed by the researcher.

Guidelines in the literature regarding human relation skills are at best vague and sometimes contradictory. They include the advice to remain an outsider as well as to become a friend, and to be totally honest about the purpose of one's presence as well as to stay as vague as possible. Reasons for these guidelines vary from ethical concerns to concern for the validity of the data.

My own position has been one of honesty both for ethical reasons and from the conviction that the subjects could understand the role of someone who wants to learn about their lives and the setting in which they live. My standard explanation for my presence to staff members as well as subjects was the following: I am a student of special education and I would like to learn how you live here and how you think about your life. The subjects' reaction was one of normal acceptance. One of the subjects, Rob, responded: "Oh, I can show you all about the place here."

During the course of the research, the personal and methodlogical field notes show that four factors regularly needed attention while interacting with the subjects: (1) the need to maintain a non–authoritative status, (2) the need to maintain a status of non–opinion giving, (3) the need to maintain clarity about my role as a student in which I could not offer any help, and

(4) the need to maintain awareness not to become personally involved.

It took continuous effort not to accept any authority the staff as well as the subjects were inclined to put on me, regardless of the fact that I had explicitly stated that I had none. The field notes note many times when subjects would ask permission to do something or go somewhere. My standard response was: I have nothing to say here, you have to ask someone else.

On several occasions, subjects (especially Dave and Terry) would ask my opinion about such issues as the possibility of getting an apartment or getting married. I was careful each time to make explicit that I had no opinion and that my interest in talking about these topics did not indicate one.

The necessity of having to maintain clarity about my inability to extend actual help is illustrated in the following segment:

> While drinking coffee with Max in the rollerskating rink, he said that he did not want to go to the cottages. I asked him why. **Max:** That is not home . . . you know what I really like? An apartment . . . a place of my own, where I can be by myself you know . . . (He had been talking to me about that several times.) **Author:** Yes, I know, but I want you to know very clearly that I cannot help you with that . . . I think I can understand it but I cannot help you get it . . . **Max:** Are you not a psychologist any more? Or an analyst? **Author:** No, I never was a psychologist or an analyst . . . I am in special education and I am not someone of the staff, I am here only to try and understand the persons who live here . . . but I cannot do anything for you . . . **Max:** "But who *can* do something for me?" (July 10, visit 28)

The fourth aspect dealt with subjects initiating personal relationships extending beyond the visitor role in which I had been cast. On two occasions, one of the male subjects asked me to dance with him when playing his records. Both times there was no one else around. I reacted by stating: Some other time perhaps, when there is a party. The personal notes on that occasion reflect a feeling of discomfort with the situation. A female subject started showing signs of attachment by hugging me upon my arrival. While I did not reject it, I did not actively respond to or initiate this behavior either. None of these situations turned into problem situations, but they kept me alert in my own affect behavior towards the subjects.

DATA ANALYSIS

A description of how the data were analyzed is rather important as this process differs from the way many qualitative studies typically have analyzed and presented data. In most cases, the findings are described and examples of these findings are provided. The reader is left uninformed of *how* the findings were extracted from the mass of data and on *how many* data the findings are based. Thus, grounds for an individual judgment of credibility and significance are lacking.

The present study has attempted to account for each step taken in the conduct of the research. A precise description of data analysis procedures was facilitated by use of Grounded Theory methodology as set forth by Glaser and Strauss (1967). Essentially, Grounded Theory methodology systematically isolates behavioral patterns in the data. The major steps in this process are (1) generation of categories and their properties, (2) theoretical sampling and theoretical saturation, and (3) isolation of behavioral patterns.

A full description of the application of this approach in the present study as well as the application of validity and reliability procedures can be read in the original report (Heshusius, 1978). For the purpose of this writing, these major steps in the data analysis are outlined below.

Generation of Categories and Their Properties

A category consists of a group of observations on a particular theme. In the present study, the observations are segments of the field notes. Within each category there are subgroups of observations indicating different meanings the subjects gave to the central theme. These subgroups are the properties of the category.

For instance, in many observations the subjects referred to marriage. These observations gave rise to the category "marriage." In these observations subjects expressed various meanings the concept of marriage held for them. These subgroups of observations, expressing different meanings of marriage, constituted the properties of the marriage category.

The actual process of category generation consisted of segmenting the field notes into individual observations that expressed opinions or emotions (through acts and/or verbal statements) about facts of past, present, or future events. For instance, the following segment states facts as well as an emotion about the facts.

> Terry tells me that Paul has another job. Now she does not see him anymore. She adds: "I miss him at work." (December 18, visit 73)

The first two sentences merely state facts. These facts deal with the subject's work situation. This, and similar observations, rendered the category "Work." The third sentence expressed a particular meaning this subject gave to work in this specific observation. This, and similar observations, gave rise to the property: "Work means contact with friends."

The process of segmenting the field notes rendered a total of slightly over 1000 observations. These observations gave rise to the following categories: boy/girl friend relationships, gender roles, having and rearing children, health, independence, interpersonal understanding, intrapersonal understanding, marriage, meeting authority with unpleasant demands, money, physical/sexual contact, sexual intercourse and nudity, religion, recreation, significant others, and work.

Next, all observations within each category were compared and sorted into the different meanings attached to the central theme of the category. This rendered the properties of the categories. The common elements of each category and each property were formulated into definitions. After a validation process and further saturation of categories and properties, these definitions formed the basis for articulating the findings.

Validity and Reliability Procedures

In the present study at least three questions can be raised when assessing the validity of the data: (1) how accurate are the category and property definitions in representing the particular observations they try to capture?, (2) how was the researcher perceived by the persons in the setting? and (3) how did other persons in the setting perceive the events in the observations? These questions of validity were respectively addressed by the process of coder validation, by describing the researcher's presentation of self, and by testing the researcher's observations against those of the subjects and other persons in the setting.

Coder validation

Two coders coded substantial samples of observations into the category and property definitions. These coders were doctoral students in psychology and were recommended by the chairperson of the special education department.

Essentially, during the process of coder validity (1) the coders coded samples of the data, using the category and property definitions; (2) discrepancies in coding between coders or between coders and myself were discussed and these discussions were tape recorded; (3) the recorded discussions were analyzed to isolate sources of discrepancies; and (4) definitions were modified as indicated by the nature of the sources of the discrepancies. This entire process was repeated until there were no further disagreements in coding decisions and the definitions could be judged adequate in representing the data in the field notes. These coding procedures took place in three sessions for a total of eleven hours.

Researcher's presentation of self

After all data were collected, four houseparents were handed a questionnaire asking their perceptions of the possible effects of the researcher's presence on the subjects' behavior. These four houseparents had been in their function during all or most of the research period. Appendix B contains the questionnaire and the actual responses. In sum these responses indicate that the researcher's presence had been seen as a rather ordinary activity.

Other persons perceptions

The researcher's perceptions of events were often checked out against the perceptions of other persons in the setting. Examples from the field notes in the substantive chapters will show how many questions of the following kind were asked: "I heard you mention . . . Is that what you mean?" Or, "I saw this or that happen yesterday.—What do *you* think of it?"

In addition, at the end of the research, the findings of the study were presented to the houseparents and their reactions were elicited. All category and property definitions and many of the observations were presented. The houseparents' reactions to the data were tape recorded. The analysis of the recording indicated a judgment of high ecological validity of the data. The houseparents stated that the study had "picked up things that are there pretty accurately." None of the findings were seen as not valid or doubtful.

Reliability

The purpose of validity coding was to establish category validity, that is, to modify category and property definitions to the point where they adequately represented the behavioral events they were designed to represent. The purpose of reliability concerns the researcher's and coder's consistency in the coding of the observations once the definitions have been established. Approximately 40 percent of all observations from which the findings emerged were used in reliability coding. Coefficients were calculated per category. Categories and their properties are reliable, given that their definitions are consistently applied to the data by multiple coders at one point in time or by one coder over time. The overall multiple and same coder coefficients were .914 and .957 respectively; coefficients ranged from .80 to 1.00 across the various categories.

Theoretical Sampling, Saturation, and Isolation of Patterns

The initial data collection was an attempt to provide an account of all that there was to see. Categories and properties were then generated and validated, and reliability procedures were carried out. After these processes, data collection became more focused. Without violating the principles of a naturalistic methodology, I started to "pick and choose" with regard to whom I would talk, about what and to what extent to probe, and where I would go for further data collection. These decisions were made in order to saturate certain categories and properties, which seemed of greatest significance relative to the scope of previous knowledge and to the amount of subjects' behavior they explained. Glaser and Strauss (1967) name this picking and choosing "theoretical sampling."

Slowly, some categories and properties became more and more saturated; others dropped out as I was not able to collect enough data on them within the boundaries of the study to render a substantial enough base from which findings could have been articulated. Clearly, data collection has to come to a stop at some point. The answer to the question, "What is enough?" is by necessity an estimation. At a certain point, certain observations occur again and again, and the researcher decides that the category or property is saturated. In other words, collecting more observations would only add bulk to the data. The following chapters will provide the reader with frequency tables indicating the number of observations collected on the categories and properties upon which the particular findings are based. Although these frequencies will provide one means for forming a judgment of confidence, they do have a relative rather than an absolute value. Clearly, the naturally occurring rate of the behaviors determine their accessibility for observation when participant observation is used as a data-gathering strategy. For instance, the touchiness of discussing the subjects' status as a mental retardate made for a low frequency count of relevant behaviors as compared to frequencies of behaviors of more casual topics of conversation. However, these comments were made in a strong and definite manner. Therefore, a few observations on this issue may be as significant as many observations on more casual topics.

While collecting data to saturate categories and properties, I started looking for relations between them. Relations between categories and properties can form patterns in the data. Thus, a pattern can be described as a set of relations between properties and categories, which can form the base from which findings can be formulated.

FORMAT OF DATA PRESENTATION

From the relations between categories and properties four clusters of patterns emerged. These four clusters dictated the nature of the following chapters, which respectively deal with independence, marriage and related issues, interpersonal understanding, and intrapersonal understanding. In each of these chapters, a diagram of the pattern is presented, then the full definitions of the categories and properties are listed, after which the pattern is more fully described. A discussion follows in which an attempt is made to integrate the findings into the scope of previous literature and in which implications for program planning and future research are suggested.

Using diagrams to portray relations between categories and properties allows the reader to follow the isolation of the pattern in a visual mode. The following symbols are used in the diagrams:

label = category

[label] = property

——► = contains the property of

—— = relation

---- = implied relation

Key words from the category and property definitions are used when labeling the properties and categories in the diagrams and in the tables. The full definitions as they were formulated after coder-validity procedures appear below the diagrams. For example, Figure 3 represents the pattern that reflects the subjects' perceptions on having and rearing children. In describing the pattern, many examples and frequency tables of observations from which the findings emerged will be provided. Where applicable, variation within the patterns and negative cases are discussed. Variations may be defined as the degree to which the categories and/or properties vary under diverse conditions (see Glaser and Strauss, 1967). In the present study, variations occurred between voluntary and elicited remarks, between observations from group setting and from the researcher-subject only setting, between the sexes, and over time.

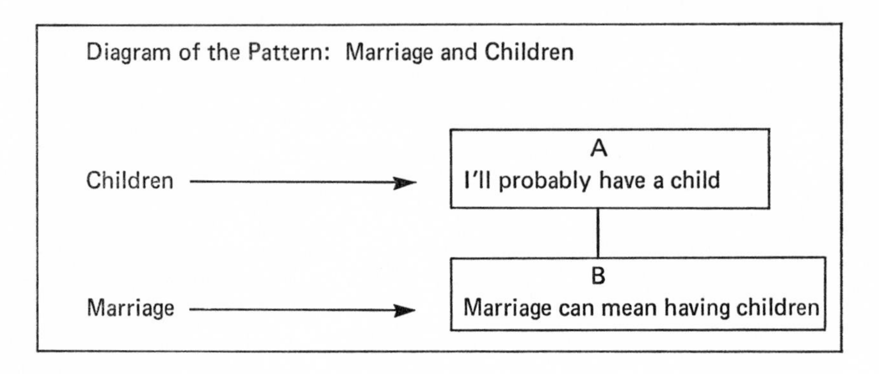

DEFINITIONS

Category: Children: Any act of verbal statement reflecting a meaning the subjects gave to having and rearing children.

Property A: Having children is seen as a possibility. One sees oneself capable of having and rearing children, if not now, then at some point in the future.

Category: Marriage: Any act or verbal statement reflecting a meaning the subjects gave to married life.

Property B: Marriage means the possibility of having children.

Figure 3.

With regard to the discussion of negative cases, one needs to keep in mind that negative cases do not necessarily disprove or debunk what has been isolated as a significant pattern for most of the behavior by most of the subjects. A negative case represents another comparative datum, which could possibly generate another property or could bring about modifications or additions or could raise questions for further research.

It might merit restating that the ample examples used are the indicators of the findings. Validity and reliability procedures ensured that regardless of which observation was chosen to be used as an example it was representative of all observations coded under the category or property it was taken from. Why one example was chosen over another had to do with its illustrative power and its contribution to covering the range of subjects, settings, and events in this research.

It should be stressed that this research does not in any way attempt to evaluate and judge abilities of subjects or staff members, nor does it attempt to state "the facts." Its central aim was to grasp some ways by which the subjects of this study made sense of their daily lives.

Chapter 3

INDEPENDENCE

THE THEME OF INDEPENDENCE constituted a major preoccupation for the subjects of this study. A desire for greater independence showed in much of what these persons did, said, and reacted to. The properties from which this pattern emerged fell into two major groups: pride in acquired independence, and desire for greater independence. This is shown in Figure 4.

Table II shows that approximately 75 percent of all statements in the observations were volunteered; this means that, on the average, one statement was volunteered every visit.

In terms of its occurrence, as well as its significance, the property "wanting to live alone, or to be on-my-own" is most interesting.

A statement indicating the desire to live on one's own was made thirty-one times. That is an average of once every third visit. Twenty-one of these comments were volunteered. Moreover, all subjects contributed to this property. Living "on-my-own" was clearly their dream and the very thought occupied them greatly. Some representative examples of this property follow.

> EXAMPLE: 1: I talked with Max in the refreshment area of the roller skating rink. We were sitting alone at a table. He said that he wanted to go home, but that he actually did not want to go to the cottage. I asked him why not. **Max:** That is not home . . . where I can be by myself, you know . . . (July 10, visit 28)

> EXAMPLE 2: At the weekly staff and male-clients meet-

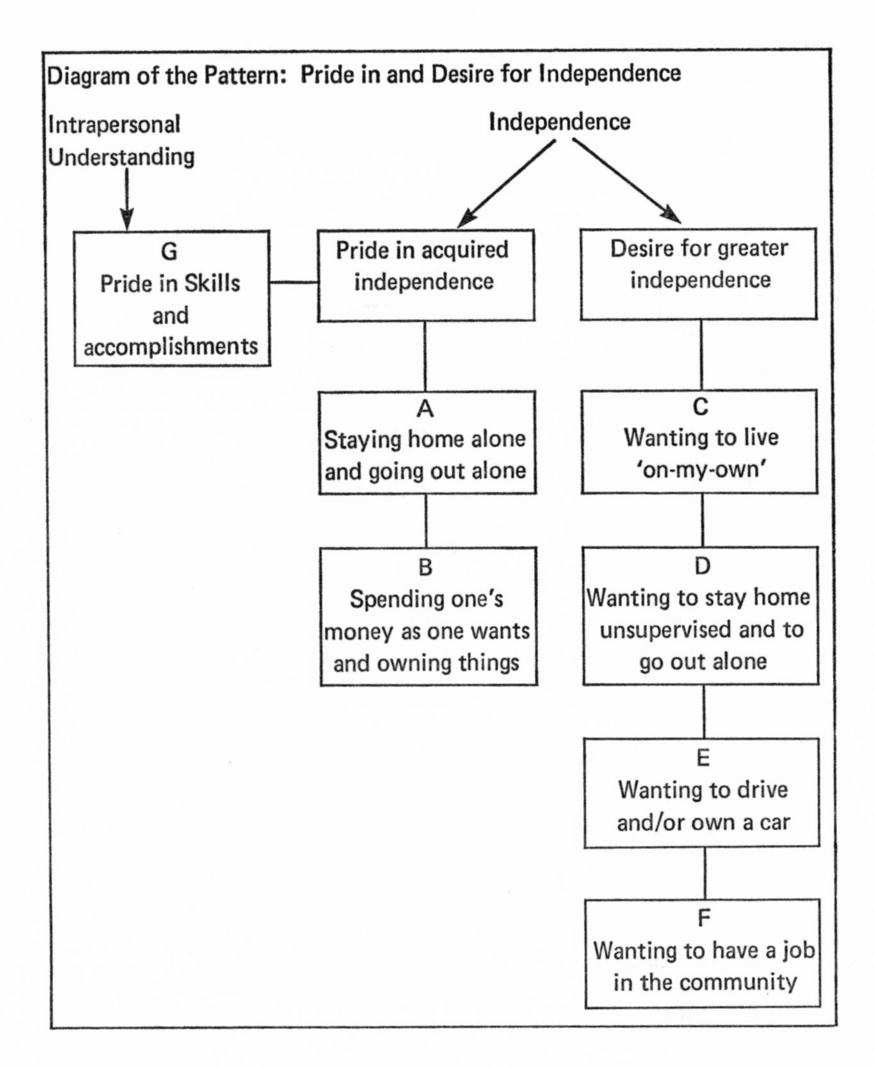

DEFINITIONS:

Category: Independence: Any act or verbal statement reflecting a meaning the subjects gave to being free or wanting to be free from control of others as they knew such control in their existing situations.

Properties: Pride in independence already acquired, such as:

A: Staying home alone and going out alone.

B: Spending one's money the way one wants to and owning things.

Figure 4.

Wanting to be independent in what one thinks oneself capable of even though it is not feasible or not allowed in the present situation.

C: Wanting to live alone, or "to-be-on-my-own."

D: Wanting to stay home unsupervised and wanting to come home and go out without having to account for it.

E: Wanting to drive and/or own a car.

F: Wanting to have a job in the community.

Category: Intrapersonal Understanding: Any act or verbal statement reflecting a meaning the subjects gave to one's own behavior: thoughts, feelings, and reflections about its limitations, boundaries, motivations, or possible consequences.

Property: Pride in one's skills, talents, or accomplishments.

(Figure 4.)

Table II

Frequency Distribution of Observations of the Pattern: Pride in and Desire for Independence

Properties	*Volunteered*	*Elicited*	*Total*
A. Staying home and going out alone	7	2	9
B. Spending money as one wants and owning things	23	5	28
C. Wanting to live alone	21	10	31
D. Wanting to stay home unsupervised and go out alone	10	5	15
E. Wanting to drive and/or own a car	12	2	14
F. Wanting to have a job in the community	3	5	8
G. Pride in skills and accomplishments	17	5	22
Total	93	34	127

ing, Don was asked by the resident coordinator (John) if he had any complaints. **Don:** "No," and shook his head. **Houseparent:** "That is a falseness . . . yesterday you told me that there were several things. How about the money?" **Don:** "That money object . . . John . . . I say . . . I got some in the bank . . . Is that going to help me

. . . John . . .?" **John:** "I am not sure what you are getting at . . . get to the point . . . what do you want to use the money for?" **Don:** "As it is . . . (mumbled something) . . . is that what you had in mind . . . John?" **John:** "Are you talking about apartments?" **Don:** "Yes!" **John:** "What specifically do you want? Do you want an apartment?" **Don:** "Yes, I do. " **John:** "Well . . . let me talk about that and explain it as simple as possible . . ." October 18, visit 57)

EXAMPLE 3: Sitting next to Don on the couch, with the television on, I asked him if there had been any further talk about getting an apartment. **Don:** "No." **Author:** But you still want one? **Don:** Yes . . . yes, but it cost money. **Author:** What is so good to you about living alone? **Don:** No one bothers me . . . no hassles . . . **Author:** Oh, you don't like to be bothered . . . **Don:** No, I don't like to be pushed around. And a little later in the conversation: "I won't stay here all my life . . . by no means" and he repeated a minute or so later again: "By no means, I won't stay here all my life." (December 15, visit 71)

EXAMPLE 4: On the way back from a concert in town which I attended with Pam, we talked about her family. I asked her if she thought she would ever live alone. She said that the houseparent, the resident coordinator, her mother and herself had had a meeting a while ago but they thought that she was not ready yet. I asked her what she thought herself. **Pam:** (Nodding her head positively) I think I can . . . maybe not right now . . . **Author:** Do you see yourself living alone in three or four years? **Pam:** "Oh yes, by then I will, I hope," and added: I think I will be better off alone than with all the others. (October 27, visit 59)

EXAMPLE 5: We are watching a story on television about a teenage daughter whose parents are too busy to pay attention to her. She then takes her baby sister and runs away. **Kitty:** (interjects) I did that once . . . Carl is now three . . . I have not seen him in a long time . . .

he may not know me anymore if he would see me now . . . (name of resident coordinator) says that sometime I may have him back. **Author:** Have your child back? **Kitty:** "Yeah . . . (nodding her head) . . . he told me that . . . when I have a place of my own some day." (August 20, visit 37)

EXAMPLE 6: I asked Rob, with whom I was chatting alone, whether he liked the cottages. **Rob:** I like it here but I would like to be on my own . . . or perhaps live with my mother . . . (August 5, visit 33)

EXAMPLE 7: **Terry:** Wayne called me last night to ask me why I had been mad at him . . . he wants to marry me . . . in a few weeks I hope . . . I want to get out of here . . . I hate it here . . . I can't stay here all my life, can I? Wayne says that too – I can't stay here all my life . . . (September 9, visit 48)

The desire "to get out of here" was not necessarily connected with not liking the actual setting. Though at times the desire was stimulated by a dislike for a specific aspect of the setting, often it merely expressed the wish for a greater degree of independence in living conditions. Also, several subjects connected the desire "to get out" with the feeling that the cottages were not quite like home. Max, in example 1, and Lisa, in example 8, express this connection:

EXAMPLE 8: I accompanied Lisa to the bank and we had coffee afterwards in one of the town's coffeehouses. I picked up on her stay with her sister over Christmas. I asked her whether she considered her sister's home as her home. **Lisa:** No, not really . . . **Author:** Is the cottage a home for you? **Lisa:** "That is a home away from home, you know what I mean?" **Author:** Are you saying that it is not a real home for you then? **Lisa:** Yes, it is not. **Author:** Would you rather live with your sister, or your mother, or alone? **Lisa:** With my mother in an apartment – or married . . . my sister says I can't live with my mother . . . we don't get along she says . . . **Author:** Is that what you think? **Lisa:** Well, at one time, but not now

> I think. Mothers and daughters have arguments, don't they . . . don't you with your daughters? Don't you sometimes want to shake them (gesturing)? But I live now by myself, really . . . "I am on my own . . . I don't live with my mother at home . . . So I am on my own . . . in a way (said with deliberation while looking as if questioning me at the same time) . . ." (January 21, visit 81)

Lisa, almost cunningly, expressed the importance of independent living by going through pains in finding a rationalization for the notion that even her present living situation reflects, at least, some degree of independence. Casually, she mentioned marriage as one way to obtain a home and greater independence.

I could not find any negative cases for this desire "to get out of here" or "to live on my own." One possible exception would be the following observation in which Jane expressed doubt about the possibility of living alone:

> EXAMPLE 9: I was talking with Kitty in her room, who told me that sometime she may have a place of her own. Jane came in and I asked her if she thought she could live alone. **Jane:** "No." I asked her why not. **Jane:** "I would pass out . . . I take pills . . . four white ones and four pink ones." **Author:** Have you ever passed out here? **Jane:** No, but I did at my mommie's house. **Author:** If you never would pass out, do you think you could live alone? **Jane:** "Yes, then I could." **Author:** Would you want to? **Jane:** Yes, would like to, alone, or with a roommate . . . (January 5, visit 77)

Jane was under great influence of her mother and grandmother, who both treated her as a child. For instance, Jane laughingly told me that her mother still gets a babysitter when she needs to go away even for a short time. Jane's own view on the issue seems to be one of desire for greater independent living and a belief in her capabilities for doing so in the face of contradictory opinions from relatives. The next observation lends support to this judgment by reflecting Jane's belief in her own capabilities:

> EXAMPLE 10: Jane entered the kitchen where Elen (houseparent), with whom I had been talking, was just leaving. Alone with Jane, she told me that Jill would be the housemother the coming weekend. She added something that I could not totally understand, but I interpreted that she did not like that. **Author:** You don't like Jill as a housemother? **Jane:** "No . . . and I don't like Candy either . . ." **Author:** Who do you like? Jane mentioned a name and then asked me whether I knew who would be the housemother when Elen left (Elen, who had been a housemother for some years, had to quit her job and would be leaving in the near future). I said I did not know. **Jane:** "I can be the housemother . . . or Lisa . . ." and added: . . . but I live here . . . (October 18, visit 57)

Often the subjects attempted to connect meanings attached to their vision of living-on-one's-own to the realities of their daily lives — as Don with regard to his money in the bank (example 2); or Kitty, with regard to her actual wish to have her child back (example 5); or Don, with being tired of being "hassled" in the actual setting (example 3); or Pam, wanting to escape from the commotion involved in always being with a group of people (example 4); or Rob and Terry wanting to be free from "being pushed around" (elsewhere in the field notes), or Max, also wanting to escape from the constant presence of people (example 1).

At other times, they merely projected themselves to be happier without connection to unpleasant particulars in their actual situation. A general trend running through the subjects' desire to live on their own was a need for privacy, expressed negatively in their annoyance with being in the constant presence of others.

Clearly the subjects' projection of a desired future was brought about by a desire to change the actual. Any projection of the future is essentially a desire to change the present, which necessitates an awareness and an evaluation of the actual. It is patent that the subjects of this study were engaged in such process of awareness and evaluation of their actual situation.

Living on one's own then, was a strong desire for the subjects in this study, whether living on one's own was visualized as completely independent, with a roommate, or as a married person. For the majority of the subjects, the most critical motive for this desire to live on one's own was the wish to be one's own boss without being hassled by others. For some, the expectation was that living on one's own would be more like a real home.

The subjects' desire to stay home alone and go out alone was another indication of the importance they attached to obtaining greater degrees of independent living. Only four persons were allowed to stay home alone or go out alone for any length of time. All four expressed pride in being able to do so.

> EXAMPLE 11: During lunch break at the workshop I chatted with Pam. I told her that I was thinking of inviting all of the persons at the cottages to my house the coming Sunday and I asked her if she wanted to come too. She told me that she was going to a friend's house. **Author:** I almost have to make an appointment with you to see you. Pam laughed. **Author:** I am serious . . . I'd like to talk to you more about your life here. **Pam:** "Here? . . . Boo . . . well, it is better now I can go out to town by myself . . . get away from the others." (September 17, visit 51)
>
> EXAMPLE 12: When visiting the women's cottage, Kitty told me that she went to the dentist ". . . all by myself and came back all by myself . . . for the first time!" She had her wisdom tooth taken care of and had to return next week. Candy, a practicum student entered the cottage. **Kitty:** "Candy . . . guess what . . . I went all alone in a cab to the dentist . . . went alone . . . the first time!" (November 9, visit 65)

The four subjects who were not allowed to stay home alone or go out by themselves expressed their desire to do so, or they stated their resentment or incomprehension at not being allowed to.

> EXAMPLE 13: Terry mentioned twice that she was going to get a new job downtown, a "new job" where she

"would be on my own." I asked her what "being on my own" meant to her. **Terry:** "Going places by myself, call the bus or cab, like Pam does." (January 19, visit 79)

EXAMPLE 14: Lisa was telling me how bad she felt when she got up. **Lisa:** This was one of these days that you wished you had stayed in bed . . . She added: I almost fainted twice today—and found myself in the nursing room. **Author:** Can't you stay at home when you don't feel well? **Lisa:** No. Elen (houseparent) told me I have to get up and go to work anyway. I asked her why she thought she could not stay home alone. **Lisa:** I guess Elen thinks "that we are not old enough." **Author:** Well . . . you are 37 . . .? What else could be the reason? **Lisa:** "Oh, she thinks we 'chise' ourselves." **Author:** What does that mean? **Lisa:** Oh, come on . . . **Author:** Seriously, I am not from this country and some words I really don't know. I don't know what chise means. **Lisa:** "She thinks we might kill ourselves or something." **Author:** Could it also be because you might have seizures? **Lisa:** Yes, it could, and then I can see her point . . . (October 13, visit 54)

Table II shows a rather high frequency (28) of observations coded under the property "spending one's money the way one wants to and owning things." All subjects were allowed to have and spend their pocket money, and all would show pride in doing so. They would often draw my attention to things they possessed, received from friends, or had just bought: clothing items, jewelry, records, tools, photo's in frames, but also major items, such as a radio, an old tape cassette recorder, a television set, and a small organ were shown. Some subjects seemed to own an enormous amount of clothing. They would show me their closets and open drawers. After Rob's grandfather died (during the period of the research) he inherited dozens of clothing items, which were all added to his already overfull closet. The only subject who never showed off his possessions to me was Don. However, Don was known to collect any junk he could find, and his room looked accordingly, filled with boxes stuffed with odds and ends.

With regard to making a living, it seems of interest that only eight observations indicated a desire to have a job in the community, and none indicated that earning money was a major motive. While, for instance, holding a job was a major concern for Edgerton's (1967) subjects, the subjects of this study barely gave it a thought. Their perceptions seemed to be that they had a job, namely the one at the workshop. The subjects did not conceptualize that the money they made would not be nearly enough to live independently. These persons had never experienced the need to make a living, nor did they understand the buying value of money.

Many times, subjects showed a pride in their accomplishments, which indicated a certain pride in being independent. They were proud of knowing the road in town; of knowing how to use a camera, to play the piano or the organ, to cook and clean, to drive a car, to read, to buy presents and clothes alone, and to use a film projector (this is not to say that all these accomplishments could have been judged adequately performed from the point of view of others).

> EXAMPLE 15: Don entered the women's cottage — almost exhilarated and more talkative than I have ever seen him. He looked very sharp. I remarked about his clothes. **Don:** (Beaming) "I bought this on the sales today . . . in the mall . . . three shirts and the pants . . . a bargain I had . . ." He hardly stuttered, as he usually does. I asked him whether he had gone there alone. He said he had. (August 20, visit 37)

There were twenty-two observations of this kind. The subjects' pride in their daily accomplishments would seem to be another indication of the importance they attached to greater independence.

Discussion

While no literature could be located on the way persons labeled retarded who live in a group home make sense out of their daily lives, several publications have noted the desire "to get out of here" by persons in institutions for the retarded (Bogdan and Taylor, 1977; Edgerton, 1967; Braginski and Braginski, 1971;

Mattinson, 1970).

While the group home certainly allowed a greater extent of participation in the mainstream of society than is the case in a total institution, the desire for independence was clearly not satisfied, nor was the need for privacy. While the subjects seem to greatly enjoy community participation, living in the group home did not equate with "being-on-my-own." The significance of this finding will be addressed in greater detail in the discussion of Chapter 4 after presenting the data on marriage and related issues.

The more narrowly defined manifestations of the desire for greater independence expressed in wanting a car and in the pride of owning things have also been noticed by other researchers. Edgerton (1967) found the automobile to be an ultimate symbol of success, but for all but a few it was an unattainable commodity because of the requirements for its legal operation and cost. Thus, Edgerton's subjects saw a car as a symbol of success. For the subjects in the present study, it seemed to be primarily a means that would bring greater independence, although, obviously, the success and status symbol may well have been part of it.

The importance of owning things was also noted by Mattinson (1970) and Edgerton (1967). Mattinson's subjects showed the observers all their possessions: they opened drawers and closets, and showed pictures and other items. Edgerton's subjects picked up souvenirs, photos, and odds and ends of all kinds in junk stores or trash cans, or borrowed them from friends and displayed them in their houses. They often would attach false tales to these items. Mail picked up from other places was on display, as well as books and magazines they could not read. Similarly, a subject of the present study, Rob, showed me several books in his room, including an entire teacher-edition of a reading method, found in the trash can of the nearby school. When I asked him whether he could read these books he said: "No, but when I get married my children can," and he added: "Don't they look good? Did I put them the right way?" (January 30, visit 83). The most parsimonious interpretation of these behaviors would seem to be the one offered by Edgerton (1967, p. 151): these items were symbols of normalcy.

While a finding such as the importance of owning things may appear not to be very important, its significance lies in increasing the understanding or the interpretive practices the other person employs in everyday living. As was noted in Chapter 1, the practicality of this sort of knowledge lies in the access it provides to the way life is seen as meaningful, which can render clearer communication. For instance, when I showed houseparents the findings of this study to obtain their perceptions, one person reacted to the importance of "owning things" as follows: "That is good to know — I was just about to clean up the cottage and getting them to get rid of their junk." Clearly, then, junk as well as beauty is in the eye of the beholder, and so is the meaning attached to it. Awareness of ways in which the other makes sense out of her/his life, even with regard to issues as "simple" as owning "junk," may prevent clashes in communication.

Chapter 4

MARRIAGE AND RELATED ISSUES

THE CONCEPT of marriage played a most important role in the subjects' lives. Marriage was valued for a variety of reasons. These persons viewed marriage as a viable possibility for their own future. They mentioned marriage in one way or another frequently.

This chapter will discuss various meanings the subjects gave to the concept of marriage. First, evidence is presented that marriage is valued and viewed as possible. Then, the patterns that reflect different meanings given to the concept of marriage are described: marriage as it relates to independent living, physical/sexual involvement, having and rearing children, and having a boy/girl friend.

POSSIBILITY AND VALUE OF MARRIAGE

This pattern was generated from relations between properties within the category Marriage, as is shown in Figure 5.

Most of the comments on the possibility and values of marriage were volunteered and elicited comments did not require much probing (Table III). The following examples are representative of these frequently occurring behaviors.

EXAMPLE 16: I am alone with Don in the living room. On television there is a movie about a married couple. I ask Don whether he sees himself married at some point. He flashes a sudden smile and says shyly: Yeah . . . possible . . . some time . . . I ask him his age. **Don:** "Twenty nine" . . . **Author:** Well, that is young enough . . . **Don:** "But what if she lives there and I here? I have her

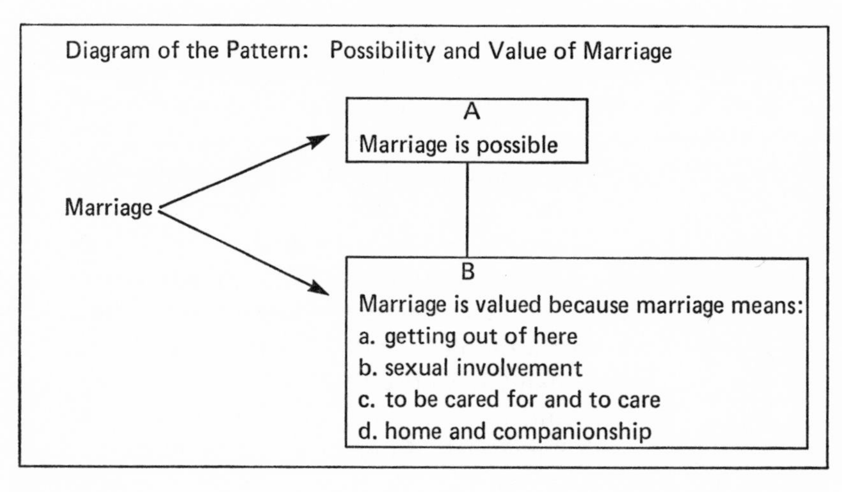

DEFINITIONS

Category: Marriage: Any act or verbal statement reflecting a meaning the subjects gave to married life.

Property A: Marriage means a possible way of life.

B: a. Marriage means independent living or a means of "getting out of here."

b. Marriage means a "go ahead" for sexual behavior in which intercourse may be implied but is not explicitly stated.

c. Marriage means being taken care of, taking care of the other, or doing things for each other.

d. Marriage means home, companionship, or happiness.

Figure 5.

Table III
Frequency Distribution of Observations of the Pattern:
Possibility and Value of Marriage

Properties	*Volunteered*	*Elicited*	*Total*
A. Marriage is possible	26	16	42
B. a. Marriage means getting out of here	10	4	14
b. Marriage means sexual involvement	7	7	14
c. Marriage means to be cared for and to care	7	1	8
d. Marriage means home and companionship	9	—	9
Total	59	28	87

phone number . . ." (in a confused way, expressing "what *do* I do?"). **Author:** Oh, you are talking about a specific girl? I meant just marriage in general . . . not necessarily with someone you know . . . but you have a specific girl in mind? **Don:** Yes. **Author:** I meant just marriage. **Don:** "When I cook I have that in mind." I asked him what. **Don:** That . . . m-a-r-r d e (trying to spell the word 'marriage'). **Author:** Marriage? **Don:** "Yes. What is your opinion?" **Author:** About what? **Don:** About getting married. **Author:** I didn't have one . . . all I am asking is what you think about it yourself. What are you talking about? **Don:** Could I save enough money to get married? **Author:** I don't know that. I don't know how much they can help you here. **Don:** "Oh, they don't have money!" (December 15, visit 71)

EXAMPLE 17: In the room are Teresa, Tony, Danny (a week guest who had fallen asleep), and myself. **Teresa:** I was really worried about Max . . . you know what I mean don't you? **Author:** "Hm," nodding my head a little. **Teresa:** Because I love him more than anyone . . . He is my boyfriend . . . I have others too, Philips, who you met Friday, and Wayne, but Max comes first . . . "I love him more than anyone . . . he is my boyfriend . . . and we get engaged soon . . . and then we'll get married. That is what boyfriend means doesn't it?" **Author:** Well, I think it means that you know each other for a while or a long time so you can find out whether you want to get married or not . . . **Teresa:** Oh, but I want to get married to Max, and he too. Then he will take care of me. (July 8, visit 22)

EXAMPLE 18: Sitting with Max in front of the cottage, I asked him whether he liked it there. ***Max:*** I like it here but they don't give me credit . . . I have my future locked for me. I'll marry Terry . . . in two years . . . in 1979. I'll work at —— (name of workshop) and we live in an apartment. (June 5, visit 7)

EXAMPLE 19: Lisa, Jane, Kitty, and I were sitting in

the living room carrying on a lively conversation. I asked Lisa whether her mother had married, as I knew about such plans. **Lisa:** No, her boyfriend moved to Tennessee. Now there is no wedding. But she'll get married sometimes —one day. **Author:** How about you? Will you too? **Lisa:** "Yes, (nodding her head) some day" and as she walked to the kitchen to get some coffee, she added: "My mother says I might get married before she does.' " (January 5, visit 77)

Belief in married life as a viable alternative for the future was expressed by all subjects, although with various degrees of intensity. While Rob, Terry, Max, Lisa, and Don consistently expressed their wish to marry, Jane and Pam were a bit more careful, albeit for different reasons.

EXAMPLE 20: Continuing the conversation in the previous example, **Author:** (To Jane) And you? **Jane:** "I can't marry" . . . **Author:** Why is that? **Jane:** "I can't read and write." **Author:** I asked her who had told her that because of that she could not marry. **Jane:** "My mom," and added: I can't cook good things either — like mashed potatoes and steak . . . **Author:** "What do *you* think though?" **Jane:** I don't know . . . **Author:** Would you want to marry? **Jane:** There is no one to marry . . . Bill has gone . . . he gave me an engagement ring, but now he is in Texas. **Kitty:** "Is he coming back?" **Jane:** No, he isn't. (January 5, visit 77)

EXAMPLE 21: During a break at work, I saw Pam alone and took the opportunity to seek her out for a talk. I told her I was glad to be able to talk with her as she so often was in her room or gone to visit relatives; we talked about life in the cottage. Pam mentioned her annoyance with the talk that goes on about boys by the other women: ". . . always about boys . . . always about boys . . . and then they need my shoulder to cry on . . ." **Author:** Are you yourself not interested in boyfriends? **Pam:** "I have enough to do with myself." **Author:** You mentioned once before that at one point you would like to have a baby and that that would mean marriage . . . **Pam:** "Oh

. . . maybe . . . but not now . . . I have my own troubles . . . I don't want also a husband's troubles." (September 12, visit 51)

As example 20 shows, Jane is under heavy influence of her mother who does not see her fit for marriage. The field notes contain two other conversations, similar to example 20. However, during a good part of this study, Jane carried on a seemingly pleasant and affectionate relation with Bill, another client in the workshop, from whom she was wearing an engagement ring. To her, that meant that she could not see anyone else and that she might marry him.

It should be noted here that in contradiction to the opinion of Jane's mother, some of the staff members judged Jane to be a rather capable housekeeper in the present setting and viewed her as a possible good housekeeper within a marriage context.

Pam (example 21) appears to be the only one who expresses consideration of the possible difficulties of married life, which caused her to put married life for herself at a vague level of possibility. However, on other occasions, Pam expressed views that indicated a more favorable attitude toward marriage. First, it allowed for having a child and second, as example 22 shows, Pam would consider marriage and was perhaps even desirous of it if there would be a potentially attractive partner:

EXAMPLE 22: Pam and I are driving back from a concert in town. We are talking about her life and I ask if she sees herself married at some point. **Pam:** "Perhaps . . ." **Author:** Or dating? Have you ever dated? Pam goes on to tell me that her mother never let her. She speaks with great resentment. I ask her if she would be interested in dating now. **Pam:** "Yeah . . . if there was anyone who I like." **Author:** Is there no one at the workshop? **Pam:** "At—(name of workshop)?!" and added: No . . . yeah . . . some of the supervisors I like . . . **Author:** So . . . you like some of the supervisors . . . **Pam:** Yes, do you know Ben? **Author:** Ben? **Pam:** No, Don, not Ben. I did not. **Pam:** "I like him . . . but he is married. **Author:** Does he like you too? **Pam:**

> Yes, he does, but he is married. **Author:** (Carefully) Some married people do date . . . **Pam:** I know . . . but I wouldn't . . . I never could marry him. (October 26, visit 59)

Thus, while at first glance Pam expressed little interest in marriage, this was so for reasons that had to do with the immediate behavioral setting, of which she was well aware.

In the search for negative cases, a few interesting observations on Terry turned up. While she certainly was the one who on numerous occasions talked about her desire and expectation to be married and actually announced a few times that she was getting married, there were four observations which indicated reservations. Three of them were of the following kind.

> EXAMPLE 23: After horseback riding with the entire group, I talked with Terry and Lisa, who were waiting at the car. **Terry:** Too bad that Max is not here. **Author:** Who is Max? **Terry:** That's my boyfriend. **Lisa:** "He is a sweetheart and Terry might marry him." **Author:** (To Terry) Oh, really? **Terry:** Yes, he asked me to marry him . . . a while ago . . . but I told him that I had to think it over . . . (May 24, visit 4)

Terry would take on the air of a very self-confident mistress who was being begged to marry by her lover. Her reservations in these observations appeared to be pseudo-ones. A more serious reservation was reflected in an observation obtained from a crisis situation:

> EXAMPLE 24: Terry had had a major blow-up with the houseparent the evening before this observation. Upon my arrival at noon, she was still in her room, in which she had locked herself. After a while, she came downstairs, with red eyes and nervous behaviors (nail biting, flushed, and about to cry again). She accepted my invitation to walk over with me to the other cottage. We first went around the building for a walk, during which she exploded about her dislike of life in the cottage. She then told me that her mom had said she should get married,

and added: But I don't want to get married . . . I want to be on my own. **Author:** You told me several times before that you wanted to get married . . . have you changed your mind? **Terry:** (After a little silence) . . . I maybe will get married . . . but not now. (July 31, visit 31)

It is interesting to note how a crisis situation changed Terry's outlook. However, during other crisis or semicrisis situations she seemed to want to marry more than ever. When she was sick, for instance, she wished for Max to come and get her to marry (Max had been sent to an institution at that time). In another similar crisis situation, as described in example 10, she also cried for Max to "get her out of here."

Example 25 presents the only observation I consider more problematic:

EXAMPLE 25: During recreation, we all are watching a film "The Human Tree Players," which portrays a population similar to the subjects of this study. Those persons had put together a stage performance, which had been filmed. After the performance, the audience was free to ask any questions they wished. One person asked what they saw themselves doing two years from now. Most women said they wanted to find a job and marry. Kitty: "Marry . . . not for me . . . never!" (July 29, visit 30)

The field notes reflect one other occasion where Kitty expressed that she was against the idea of marriage, though without stating why. Kitty was conspicuously absent from all forty-five observations dealing with value aspects of marriage. Only once, on being probed, did she indicate that marriage was perhaps a possibility for her:

EXAMPLE 26: While talking with Lisa and Jane about marriage I asked: How about you Kitty? Would you ever marry – do you think? **Kitty:** "I don't know . . . perhaps some day (smiling a little)." (January 5, visit 77)

However, it may well be that Kitty's consent was an artifact of the situation: I had been talking with Linda and Jane about their views of marriage, and Kitty, in a very pleasant mood that day, seemed to be agreeable to everything. The methodological notes that day reveal that Kitty was unusually pleasant and agreeable.

While Kitty's attitude toward marriage is a negative case, her extreme background—which deviates in its particular nature from the backgrounds of other subjects—highly likely accounts for this. Kitty's family story is one of poverty, alcoholism, fights, physical abuse, and sexual abuse. Kitty was "handed to relatives and neighbors for sexual use" (quote by staff member). She has a three-year-old child who was adopted by persons unknown to Kitty.

Given the extreme circumstances of Kitty's background, her unrepresentativeness should not be considered to invalidate this pattern for the population under consideration.

As stated earlier, the subjects gave various meanings to the concept of marriage. Four of these meanings were particularly distinct.

First, marriage means independent living or a means of "getting out of here."

> EXAMPLE 27: Terry tells me that her caseworker had said that it would be better to move out and marry . . . that she would be a lot happier. **Author:** But you have to have someone to marry . . . don't you? **Terry:** I have Wayne . . . he kisses me goodbye every day." **Author:** Does that mean that you may marry him? **Terry:** Yes, he asked me again today . . . and then I'll move out of here. . . (January 19, visit 79)

Second, marriage means a "go ahead" for sexual behavior in which intercourse may be implied but is not explicitly stated.

> EXAMPLE 28: I am alone with Don in the living room. On the television is a movie about a married couple. We talk about the possibility of marriage for him and he indicates his own desire to marry (with a specific girl friend). The couple on television in the meantime has progressed into bed, while necking heavily. **Author:** How about what they do, Don, would that be part of your marriage? Without looking at me, he nods yes. **Author:** And

what if you would not marry, but live in an apartment by yourself and have your girlfriend over? **Don:** "No, I couldn't . . . only when I'll be married." **Author:** Why is that? **Don:** "I don't know . . ." **Author:** Well, why do you think? **Don:** "I don't know" . . . and he persists in his usual silence. (December 15, visit 71)

Third, marriage means being taken care of, taking care of someone, or doing things for each other.

EXAMPLE 29: Lisa is talking about her sister. She mentions that her sister thinks it better for Lisa to live in the cottages: "My sister's husband is my guardian you know." She adds: They think that if I would live alone I might get sick and no one would take care of me . . . maybe that's why I want to get married . . . someone to take care of me . . . if I would be sick . . . and I would not get lonely . . . (January 21, visit 81)

Fourth, marriage means home, companionship, or happiness.

EXAMPLE 30: Rob and I are sitting in the living room of the cottage. Rob has just played one of his records and offers me a cup of coffee. He takes one himself, sits down on the couch. **Rob:** If I would be married I would be the happiest man in town (clapping his hands and laughing. We had talked before about his prospects on marriage). **Author:** Yeah, you would . . . What would you be doing now? **Rob:** I would sit here with her . . . lights out and candles on . . . soft music (laughing a little). **Author:** When do you see that happening? **Rob:** When the right girl comes along . . . I would not beat her . . . I would open doors for her and things like that . . . (July 3, visit 17)

While the meanings related to marriage of care, home, and companionship were expressed by certain subjects only, the independence and sexual involvement values were noted by all subjects. These latter values gave rise to sufficiently saturated patterns of behavior and will be discussed separately later in this chapter.

The subjects' views on the different values of marriage were intertwined with their estimation of the possibility of marriage. Often, one could not clearly distinguish between these two aspects, and it may be speculated that the subjects could not either. Therefore, valuing marriage and viewing marriage as a possibility seemed to be mutually reinforcing.

Discussion

The subjects' view of marriage as a desirable and possible state of life does raise some questions. What is the real possibility of marriage for these subjects? Is their desire for marriage typical for similar populations? Is there any evidence that marriage for them could be a viable alternative? If so, we may have to start taking their perspective more seriously and consider marriage with them in the planning and implementation of rehabilitation programs.

In 1973, Mattinson wrote that there was little if any information on marriages of "subnormal" persons. The literature provides us with few accounts indeed. The very thought of a person labeled retarded entering the institution of marriage seems a strange one for most people. As Meyers (1978, p. 107) states: "It is a mark of how little is popularly known about mental retardation today that several otherwise well-informed people asked me, after the newspaper series I wrote on Roger and Virginia for the *Washington Post,* if they were the first mildly retarded couple ever to get married."

There is enough evidence that persons of the population we label retarded do marry. Farber (1968) notes a study in which 56 percent of 1335 persons married. Of forty-eight expatients of a state hospital (Edgerton, 1967), thirty had married, which is 62 percent. Twelve of these thirty persons had married a spouse likewise labeled retarded, and eighteen (16 women and 2 men) had married an unlabeled person. Of Henshel's (1972) sample, twenty-one of the fifty-four subjects (40%) married.

Gebhard (1973) found that 25 percent of eighty-four males who were judged retarded, and who had been interviewed at the Institute for Sex Research at Indiana University, had married. These eighty-four persons had IQ scores between 31 and 70. The original sample of Mattison's (1970) study consisted of forty married couples. All eighty spouses had been discharged from the hospital; they had been variously labeled "subnormal," "feeble minded," or "imbeciles." Their IQ scores ranged from 30 to 99, the majority falling in the 50–70 range. Eleven of these eighty married persons scored between 40 and 49.

Edgerton's (1967) and Henshel's (1972) married subjects respectively covered an IQ range of 47 to 85, and 55 to 75. The background of all these subjects and their IQ scores are very similar to the subjects of the present study (see Appendix A).

Edgerton (1967), Mattinson (1970), and Meyers (1978) all found that getting married was a vital concern for their subjects. The authors attributed this concern to the fact that marriage was seen as an accomplishment, fitting the expectations for normalcy. This is most pointedly expressed by Meyer's (1978, p. 100) subject who at his wedding told the pastor who married him and his retarded wife: "Tell them (the wedding guests) that getting married is like coming out of retardation." One of Edgerton's (1967, p. 154) subjects expressed this linkage between marriage and normalcy as follows: "Before I was married I never used to have the same kind of life as other people. I was left out of so many things. Now that I got my wife (an ex-patient) I feel like I'm OK. I feel like I am just as good as anybody."

Marriage thus reinforced their newly won status as a free and full member of the outside world, which greatly enhanced their self-esteem. Henshel (1972), on the other hand, found that marriage was considered a state of life into which one naturally drifts. Though a very important status, matrimony was seen as the natural outcome of reaching adulthood. This difference seems intriguing, given the fact that Henshel's subjects had never been institutionalized, while the subjects of Edgerton, Mattinson, and Meyers had been. Three of the subjects of the present study had been previously institutionalized in a total institution and five had not. All had in common with Edgerton's, Mattinson's, and Meyer's subjects that they had been judged incompetent and not capable of managing their own affairs to the point of having to be placed in a supervised setting. This could indicate that placement in an institution or group home may make marriage extra important as a way to regain an independent place in the mainstream of society and thus to prove oneself competent in managing one's own affairs. Marriage, after all, is a socially accepted way of managing one's life through cooperation with and help from another; such help is not identified as lacking competency. Perhaps, it was also the awareness of this accepted way of managing one's affairs that led the subjects of this study to desire marriage and to equate marriage with "being on my own."

Among the subjects of both Edgerton and Henshel, the choice of spouse appeared almost random. Edgerton (1967) comments that his subjects, although opting for a mate from "the outside," would be satisfied to marry anyone, even another ex-patient.

How adequate were these marriages, referred to in the above studies? The evaluation by subjects as well as researchers is surprisingly positive. In terms of permanency, the following is of interest: of the thirty married persons of Edgerton's (1967) study, four had divorced; of Mattinson's (1970) forty couples, four had divorced; and of Henshel's (1972) twenty-one married subjects, five had divorced. Gebhard (1973), on the other hand, found a divorce rate of 63 percent among twenty-one male subjects.

Edgerton (1967) does not provide us with a systematic evaluation of his subjects' marriages, but concludes:

> Some of these marriages between former patients are happy, while others are obviously less so . . . The most important fact is that they have endured, and at the time of the research, all gave signs that they would continue to do so. (P. 119) . . . In conclusion, it would seem that the sexual and marital lives of these retarded persons are more "normal" and better regulated than we could possibly have predicted from a knowledge of ther pre-hospital experiences and their manifest intellectual deficits. And even this cursory view of their lives makes it clear that no simple stereotype can be applied to them (P. 126).

Henshel (1972), who conducted interviews, rated each spouse "low," "average," or "high" in terms of "expressed marital happiness." Thirteen couples scored "high," nine were rated "average," and six couples were rated "low." Henshel provides short summaries of the marital relations, containing some quotes by the subjects that seemed in accordance with the above range of ratings.

Mattinson (1970) directly addressed the effect of marriage. Without doubt, she positively answers the initial research question: Is marriage a viable proposition for the retarded and their children? Mattinson informally interviewed thirty-six couples who had married after their individual discharges from the hospital. Most families were visited three times, some as often as seven times, some only one time. Mattinson suggests an interesting hypothesis to account for the satisfaction of these marriages: the complementary nature of these marriages by the less competent. Says Mattinson (1970, p. 201) :

> I was particularly impressed by the mutual help these husbands and wives gave to each other and by the complementary nature of the partnerships. Recognizing their own intellectual and emotional limitations, they used their partner for what they could not do nor express for themselves. Singly, they once showed themselves to be defective in social living; paired, with renewed motivation to succeed and more often than not reinforcing each other's strengths, many of them establishing marriages which were by no means defective.

Mattinson's conclusion is summarized by scores given to each couple rating the quality of the marital relationship. Twenty-five couples rated in the two categories: "Supportive and affectionate partnership, not destructive, better married than single" (19 couples) , and "Affectionate partnership, not regretted, considerable stress, but better married than single" (6 couples) . Seven couples were rated unsatisfactory adjustment because of too heavy dependency or negative ties.

The complementary nature, suggested by Mattinson (1970), was directed primarily at the management of daily affairs. In addition, Mattinson found that the satisfaction that came from being able to help each other was "enormous." Some quotes from Mattinson's (1970) subjects are illustrative:

> "As I say, I think I'm being compensated, really, for the years before" (p. 129). "Well, we're both on the same level. I help him and he helps me" (p. 131). "I'm much better off now I'm married, but I wasn't before, was I, dear?" . . . "I'm much better off, too." "Yes, we are. I'd rather be as we are any time" (p. 132). "Well, it's had its up and downs like everybody else's, but we've always pulled back together again" (p. 135). "He doos the reading, and I doos the writing" (Mattinson, 1973, p. 181).

Most of the subjects felt lucky that they had found a mate. In accounting for the success of most of these marriages, Mattinson (1970) also refers to the fact that the initial expectations had not been too high. In addition, Mattinson suggests that the accomplishment of managing daily affairs was more important than the subtleties of life for which more competent partners wish. To be able to manage their own affairs unsupervised appeared to be most crucial in these expatients' lives.

Mattinson (1970) notes another characteristic of many of these marriages: the notion of friendship and companionship between the spouses. Edgerton (1967), too, comments on this positive component of many of the marriages of his subjects. Henshel (1972, p. 199) concludes that there may have been a greater degree of companionship than is usually found among spouses of the same socioeconomic background.

In sum, according to subjects' as well as researchers' evaluations, these studies show that marriage for persons of the population we label retarded seems to work. Marriage allowed many of these persons to manage their daily affairs together adequately. In addition, it provided companionship and friendship, factors that typically are not considered in studies of community adjustment, though such factors may well be of greater importance to the subjects than criteria such as independence and job stability. Edgerton and Bercovici (1976), for instance, found in their follow-up study of Edgerton (1967) that the subjects considered variables related to psychological well-being as major criteria of adjustment, while the researchers' criteria were of social competence and independence.

The relation between the literature discussed above and the findings of the present study consists of the following: first, the subjects' strong desire for marriage and their belief in its possibility gains credibility as a viable and valid desire; second, marriage may offer a socially acceptable way to independence-with-help, and to regain together a place in the community.

The complementary hypothesis of marriage may well be reflected in the subjects' view of marriage as valuable and possible. I came across Mattinson's (1970) work after I had stopped data collection. As I read about Mattinson's complementary hypothesis, several observations from my own data came to mind that reflected this hoping for and counting on mutual help. In total I found eight observations, of which the following are examples.

EXAMPLE 31: **Terry:** Oh, but I want to get married to Max, and he too . . . then he will take care of me and I of him. Now he takes care of me as my boyfriend and I take care of him. He does a good job and Max says I do a good job taking care of him. (July 9, visit 22)

EXAMPLE 32: Rob and I were talking about marriage. **Author:** What if your wife would want to work, would that be OK with you? And you stay home and do the housework? **Rob:** That would be fine with me. **Author:** Would you cook? I have seen you cooking here the other day. **Rob:** Yes, if we would come home from work, all washed out, then — "it is too much to clean the house *and* to cook . . . we can take turns." (May 23, visit 2)

It may be worthwhile to speculate that the desire for marriage may well be partially influenced by these persons' intuitive feeling: I do want to get out of here and be on my own—alone I can't make it but together with someone I may.

The above discussion is not to naively suggest marriage for the population we label retarded. It is to focus on a way of life for them that may offer a positive alternative. Future research further addressing the question for whom and under what circumstances marriage may be beneficial seems to be of high priority given the rather positive evaluation of existing marriages by spouses and researchers alike.

The question why marriage for persons labeled retarded has not been facilitated in any systematic way (rather, it is probably safe to say that it has been discouraged by parents as well as professionals regardless of normalization principles) must have to do with several factors. The study of these factors would be an important research concern if marriage ever has a chance to be considered a viable proposition in the systematic planning and implementation of rehabilitation programs. Two issues, which may have contributed to the absence of serious and systematic consideration of marriage for the retarded population, relate to beliefs and attitudes around "sexuality for the retarded" and to concerns with regard to having and rearing children. These issues will be addressed later in this chapter in relation to the data of the present study.

MARRIAGE AND INDEPENDENT LIVING

When comparing the data of the categories Independence and Marriage, it became apparent that getting married was seen as one way to become independent. Figure 6 reflects this small but interesting pattern.

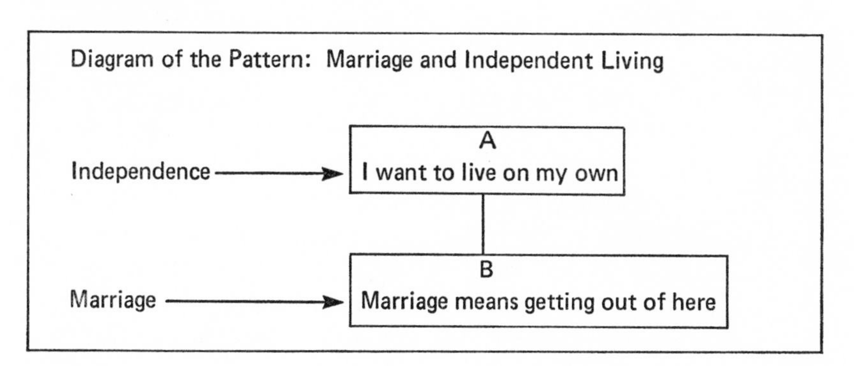

DEFINITIONS

Category:	Independence: Any act or verbal statement reflecting a meaning the subjects gave to being free or wanting to be free from control of others as they knew such control in their existing situation.
Property A:	I want to live on my own
Category:	Marriage: Any act or verbal statement reflecting a meaning the subjects gave to married life.
Property B:	Marriage means independent living or a means of "getting out of here."

Figure 6.

Fourteen of the thirty-one observations indicating the desire to "live-on-my-own" explicitly mention marriage as a means to such an end. Ten of these fourteen statements were volunteered. The examples below illustrate how living independently was almost matter-of-factly linked to the prospects of marriage:

EXAMPLE 33: When talking with Max on the picnic bench in front of the cottage, I asked him how he liked living there. **Max:** I like it here but they don't give me credit. **Author:** What do you mean by credit? **Max:**

Well, they don't give me credit. But I have my future locked for me. I'll marry Terry . . . in two years . . . in 1979. I'll work at ——— (name of workshop) and we live in an apartment . . . under supervision of ——— (name of resident coordinator). **Author:** Have you talked about these things with him or with anyone else? **Max:** No I haven't. **Author:** Would you want to? **Max:** Yes. **Author:** What seems good about being married? **Max:** I get credit . . . live by myself, with Terry . . . later in the conversation I asked him whether he could go out alone. He could. I asked whether he had to tell the houseparents where he was going or what time he would be back. **Max:** Oh, yes. That I hate to have to tell where I am going! I want to be by myself . . . get credit for me. I don't want to have to tell them where I am going. Two more years . . . I have it all figured out for myself! (June 5, visit 7)

EXAMPLE 34: Rob walked me to the car. He had just visited his mother. I asked how the stay had been since he had returned earlier than had been planned. **Author:** Wasn't it a nice visit? **Rob:** "It is sad to come here. This is not my home, you know. When I get married, that will be good . . . I might marry Teresa." **Author:** Oh, the Teresa from the workshop? **Rob:** Yeah . . . **Author:** How long have you known her? **Rob:** I met her last summer. I am going to look for an apartment soon. **Author:** How are you going to pay for that? **Rob:** We'll both work. (September 3, visit 45)

EXAMPLE 35: Terry tells me that her boyfriend asked her again to marry him, and immediately added: Then I'll move out of here . . . last year Mary (a former client) moved out of here and she lives on her own now. (January 19, visit 79)

While the subjects viewed marriage as one way to independence, staff members excluded the concept of marriage in portraying to the subjects independent ways of living. On several occasions I witnessed staff members talk to Don and Rob about the need to learn certain skills for future independent living. For instance the field notes reflect how Rob was reminded that when living by himself, he would get hungry if he forgot to take meat out of the freezer. Such reminders were used by some staff members to get the subjects to be punctual in carrying out their chores. Promises were made to both Rob and Don, in particular, but according to two staff members, these subjects had become discouraged because nothing concrete was happening. These staff members expressed their own dissatisfaction as ". . . these guys are ready."

Other subjects, too, were encouraged in their desire for independent living. For example, Terry once approached me excitedly with a piece of paper in her hand: an ad from the local paper listing an apartment for rent. She said that a staff member had indeed provided the ad. However, Terry had been told not to call, since she was not quite ready to live on her own. Thus, while the subjects' desire for greater independent living was explicitly encouraged, the idea of marriage never was.

Discussion

The marriage-independence equation by most subjects becomes of interest when comparing their perspective with the literature. While professionals encourage greater independence (vocational skills, holding a job, self-care, home care, etc.) according to normalization principles, they do not encourage or systematically facilitate marriage. From a planning and programming perspective, marriage and independence are conceptually separated. However, this separation between marriage and independence did not exist in the way the subjects of this study gave meaning to the concepts "independence" and "being normalized." On the contrary, marriage seemed to be a critical ingredient for most.

MARRIAGE AND PHYSICAL/SEXUAL INVOLVEMENT

One significant meaning given to marriage by all subjects was the physical/sexual involvement it promised. Most subjects engaged in physical intimacies such as holding hands, kissing, and hugging, but more intimate degrees of sexual intimacies and intercourse were not allowed; during the period of the research, no one, as far as can be known, engaged in them.

Several categories and properties contributed to a pattern that relates marriage to two distinct degrees of physical intimacy: sexual intercourse and the element of tease and challenge. Figure 7 attempts to represent these relations.

The most striking feature of this pattern was the subjects' strong stand on the need to be married in order to engage in more intimate degrees of physical contact and intercourse. This is not to say that these persons would not engage in these behaviors outside of marriage if their situation would allow them. In the subjects' behavioral setting, however, there was continuous and rather strict supervision and rules against sexual involvement.

Table IV shows a total of twenty-two observations pertaining to the forbidden nature of sexual involvement before marriage. This means an average of one observation every fourth visit. Given the restrictions and inhibitions put on the subjects by the behavioral setting on their expression of and engagement in sexual behavior, these twenty-two observations seem significant.

The behavioral setting was not conducive to serious discussions about sexuality. For instance, at staff meetings the issue of sex would be brought up from time to time, but in connection with practical matters of restriction. When I asked the several houseparents, only one of them mentioned that he had had serious talks about sexual behavior with the men. According to the resident coordinator, the subjects had "gleaned by themselves what they know about it." It was added that at one time or another subjects may have seen a film or book, but that there had been no program deserving the label sex-education to which one could trace back the subjects' views.

I did ask permission to talk with the subjects about these issues, and to have a portfolio on "human sexuality for the retarded" around. Permission was granted with the request to tell the houseparents what the subjects had said, so the staff would also know.

It seems safe to speculate that it may have been the very fact that I was not a staff member, and that the subjects were clear about my authority-free and nonevaluative status, that encouraged them to feel somewhat freer to speak with me about these issues. At the same time, I clearly was not one of them, and I can only

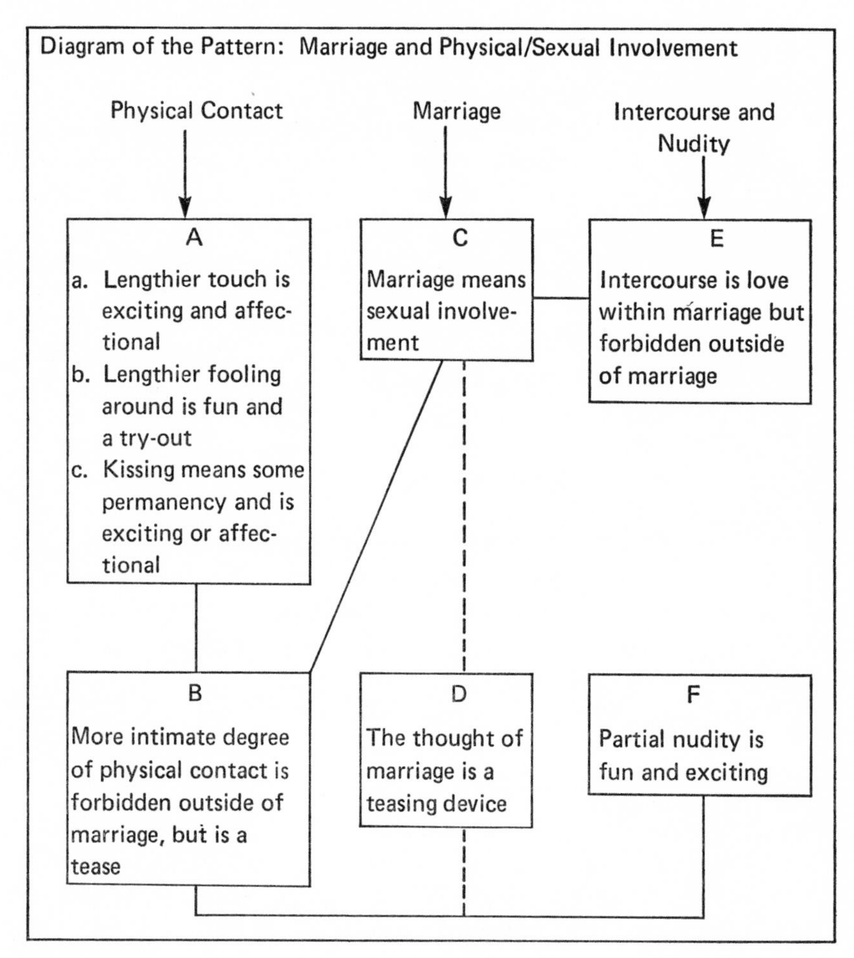

DEFINITIONS

Category: Heterosexual Physical Contact: Any act or verbal statement reflecting a meaning the subjects gave to different degrees of physical touch.

Property A:
a. Lengthier touching (stroking, embracing, hugging, holding, and cuddling beyond momentary touch) with no resistance by the receiver and no intent to challenge by the actor means excitement, pleasantness, or affection.
b. Lengthier fooling around (tickling, slapping the buttocks, pushing more than momentarily) with intent to challenge by the actor and encouraging resistance by the receiver means fun and/or trying out sexual contact without binding consequences.

Figure 7.

c. Kissing means a bond of exclusivity and permanency, is related to the boy/girl friend or husband/wife relationship, and carries the meanings of affection and excitement.

B: More intimate degree of physical contact (such as unzipping a woman's dress, touching thighs, holding tightly beyond a a short embrace or hug, sitting on one's lap or between one's legs, and reference to "hanky-panky stuff"), means a "no-no" outside of marriage, which can get you into trouble, but which also creates an exciting tension and, therefore, can be used as a teasing device.

Category: Marriage: Any act or verbal statement reflecting a meaning the subjects gave to married life.

Property C: Marriage is a "go ahead" for a high degree of physical/sexual involvement in which intercourse may be implied but is not explicitly mentioned.

D: The thought of marriage can bring about a tension expressed in nervousness or in the use of the marriage concept as a teasing device.

Category: Intercourse and Nudity: Any act or verbal statement reflecting a meaning the subjects gave to (1) sexual intercourse, and (2) nudity, defined as any degree of undress that elicits a reaction.

Property E: Intercourse means love within marriage and is part of marriage. Intercourse outside of marriage is forbidden.

F: Partial nudity carries various meanings: fun, excitement, being sexy, and has the air of "forbidden fruit."

(Figure 7.)

speculate to what extent they expressed to me their strict views on sex within marriage because of my "visitors" status. I doubt, however, that my presence totally determined their expressions, given the ease and trust that had developed between us, so that they did not feel the need to totally conform to the staff's values in relating to me. Observations in which some subjects expressed themselves quite openly (especially towards the end of the research) would support this opinion.

Table IV

Frequency Distribution of Observations of the Pattern: Marriage and Physical/Sexual Involvement

Properties	*Volunteered*	*Elicited*	*Total*
C. Marriage means sexual involvement			
B. More intimate degrees of physical contact are forbidden outside of marriage, but are a tease	6	8	14
E. Intercourse is love within marriage but forbidden outside of marriage	2	6	8
	8	14	22
A. a. Lengthier touch is exciting and affectional	—	—	23
b. Lengthier fooling around is fun and a try-out	5	3	8
c. Kissing means some permanency and is exciting or affectional			
F. Partial nudity is fun and exciting	13	9	22
	18	12	53
D. The thought of marriage is a teasing device	18	2	20
Total	44	28	95

When asking houseparents' reactions to the data, they were in agreement with the observations on the subjects' moralistic stand, which placed more intimate sexual behaviors and intercourse within the context of marriage.

Also, and more importantly so, the likelihood of their dream of greater independence coming true was contingent upon their behavior. Abstinence from sexual involvement was a strong explicit and implicit value placed on life in the cottages and in the workshop and, therefore, may have been internalized by the subjects in their eagerness to "be on their own."

EXAMPLE 36: At the beach, Terry and Max are sitting

on a big blanket in the company of Lisa and myself. Terry is in a bikini and Max in regular clothes. Terry continuously tries to cuddle up to him. Max seems a bit nervous and tries to keep Terry somewhat at a distance by saying: Give me more room, and, Terry watch out! (when she almost climbed on his lap). Yet, he holds her hand, and they talk with their faces close, and Max has a smile on his face I had not seen before. They tickle each other. **Terry:** "You want to fight?" **Max:** "No, marry" (with a smile). **Terry:** (Lowers the strap of her bikini top, because) "It is cooler . . ." **Max:** "Take it all off!" **Terry:** "We are not married yet" (with a slightly embarrassed smile). (May 30, visit 6)

EXAMPLE 37: Jane, who has been visiting her mother in Texas for a few weeks, has come back and is telling us (Lisa and myself) that her mother has a boyfriend. **Jane:** "Guess what I saw?" **Lisa:** "What?" **Jane:** "My mommie and her boyfriend kissing each other . . . in the bedroom!" And she added: I opened the door and they were kissing each other. **Author:** He is her boyfriend, isn't he? **Jane:** Yes. **Author:** Do you think they can't do that? **Jane:** "We can't . . . at ——— (name of workshop). You can't even hold hands!" **Lisa:** "You can't even go (gesturing a slap on one's bottom) or anything!" **Author:** What if you lived alone, say in an apartment. Could you then kiss your boyfriends? **Lisa:** Oh, yes, then you could hug and kiss. **Author:** Could you sleep with him and make love too? **Lisa:** No, that you can't! You are not married. **Jane:** No, you can not do that when you are not married. **Author:** Why is that? Both shrugged their shoulders but did not answer. (January 5, visit 77)

EXAMPLE 38: In the car on the way to a restaurant (where we all went to eat) Rob was alone with me. He told me that his girl friend at the workshop was pregnant; at least, he had heard about it. He added: "I don't believe it. That is nothing for her to do." **Author:** You know how one gets pregnant? **Rob:** "Oh yes, I know all about that." **Author:** So, you are not the father then? **Rob:** "Lous! No!" **Author:** Well, since she is your girl friend . . . that is the only reason why I asked. **Rob:** "No! We aren't married!" (August 16, visit 36)

EXAMPLE 39: Terry is talking to Lisa about visiting Wayne (boyfriend) in his house. **Terry:** "Then he can't sleep with me since we are not married, can he." **Lisa:** "No, he sure can't." **Terry:** Then I'll say: "Wayne, I sleep here and you there! So you can't do hanky panky stuff with me." **Lisa:** No, not until you are married. (September 20, visit 54)

EXAMPLE 40: At a party for the Fourth of July, the men come over to the women's cottage and things get livelier. Everyone is talking, laughing, joking, and making popcorn. Max and Terry fool around for quite awhile and stay close together all evening. Max slaps Terry's buttocks several times, unzips her dress a little, touches her thighs (she is wearing a rather short dress that pulls up when she sits). **Terry:** "Max! No!" (to Jane:) "That is a no no, isn't it." And later in the kitchen, when standing with Max, Max pulls her close and holds her tight. **Terry:** "Max, no, we aren't married!" **Jane:** "That is right; you aren't married. Watch out!" (July 3, visit 18)

EXAMPLE 41: In talking with Pam, on the way back from a concert in town, Pam mentioned that she would like to date a certain supervisor in the workshop, but that he was married. Therefore, she would not date him because she could never marry him. I told her that I was interested in her thoughts about lovemaking, whether that could be engaged in before marriage. **Pam:** (Looking up at me) No, I wouldn't. **Author:** And after you would be married? **Pam:** "Yes, then it is all right I guess." **Author:** Why do you believe you shouldn't before you are married? **Pam:** I don't know, you just don't. **Author:** Who tells you so? **Pam:** "It just is so." **Author:** But some people do. **Pam:** I know, but I wouldn't. (October 26, visit 59)

On several occasions I would probe for subjects' reasons behind their strict stand on marriage and sexual behavior. The general response was that they didn't know; one just didn't do that (see example 37 and 41). Two subjects did provide a specific answer. Interestingly, their reference was to religion. It may be important to note that these subjects made the connection with religion after extensive probing on my part. The question whether this indicates a possible rationalization on their part (they may have felt they had to come up with something) or whether the probing brought out some strongly conditioned attitudes will have to stay unanswered. There are not enough data to warrant either conclusion. Nevertheless, the examples are interesting.

Example 42: Rob had had a physical fight with Tim (a male resident of the cottage, but not a subject of this study) pushing him back into the shower. Tim had come out of the shower, totally nude. Rob forcefully had pushed him back. **Rob:** "He can't come out of the shower with no towel on. I want to teach him that." **Author:** Why can't he? Rob laughed. **Author:** Seriously, why can't he? I am interested in what you think about these things, about whatever I see here. **Rob.** "I know that. Well, I have been taught that way." **Author:** Why do you think it is wrong? **Rob:** "You just don't do that." **Author:** There are plenty of people around who do and who don't think it is wrong. **Rob:** Oh, yes, I know, but my mom taught us that way. **Author:** But can you say why *you* think it is wrong? **Rob:** "Well, we are created in His image" (looking up at me). **Author:** I see, that interests me much. So you think that God would not like that. Rob nodded yes. **Author:** How about when you would be married? **Rob:** "Also, I would always put a towel around me . . . all the time." **Author:** How about your wife? **Rob:** She too, wear a night gown or something. **Author:** How about in bed? **Rob:** Wear a pajama! [He reacted spontaneously without giggling or shyness which made me go on comfortably.] **Author:** How about when you make love? Would that be part of marriage? **Rob:** "Oh, yes, now I am not ready yet. I am not married . . . have no wife." **Author:** Sure, but after you would be married. **Rob:** "Oh yes, I would say: 'Come into bed!" (making a sweeping gesture). **Author:** You would have to take your pajamas off, or not? **Rob:** Sure, then we would, but I am not ready now. I have never done it . . . well once. **Author:** Oh, when was that? **Rob:** With my cousin (laughing, clapping his hands) but that was a long time ago . . . too long to remember . . . and my mother does not know, but that was the only time . . . The conversation ended here, as the houseparent called Rob in for supper. We had been talking outside in front of the cottage. (November 3, visit 62)

EXAMPLE 43: I had accompanied Lisa to the bank, after which we had a cup of coffee. While driving back to the cottage, she told me that once at a state institution where they went to play basketball she walked by accident into a men's restroom where a man was busy doing "his thing." I asked whether he seemed upset about it or not. **Lisa:** I don't think so. **Author:** Were you? **Lisa:** Not really. **Author:** Have you ever seen a man without clothes on? **Lisa:** "No . . . well, yes, in the movies. I saw *The Graduate*. That was awfully dirty." I asked her why that was so. **Lisa:** Well, he takes his clothes off and she does too. I asked what her name was and that I read the book but never saw the movie. **Lisa:** "Mrs. Robinson." **Author:** So, you think that is dirty. **Lisa:** Yes, you can't do that. **Author**: Well, what if you lived in an apartment with your boyfriend? Could you do those things? **Lisa:** I don't know. You can kiss and hug. **Author:** Can you make love then? Do you know what lovemaking is? **Lisa:** "Yes, I have seen pictures of it." **Author:** Some people do that too when they are not married. What do you think about that? **Lisa:** "That would not look good." I had to reflect for a moment about her answer before I could ask her: "Would not look good . . . to whom?" **Lisa:** "Would not look good to God. He would frown upon it" and added: He would say . . . hey, you are not married yet. "There are two people you have to listen to in your life: God and your mother." **Author:** Oh, God and your mother . . . **Lisa:** Yes (nodding her head). (January 21, visit 81)

These examples illustrate that physical intimacy and intercourse were "forbidden fruits" to be enjoyed when married. The subjects looked forward to them with anticipation and excitement as well as with some tension. It was something denied to them, yet it held a promise. It is something unknown for most subjects, referred to by them on several occasions as "hanky panky." The unknown and the forbidden aspect of sexual involvement created some tension and perhaps even some fear. Terry expresses these combined feelings of tension, fear, and attraction most clearly in example 44 when she realized that intercourse was needed in order to get the baby she wanted:

Example 44: In the living room I am sitting next to Terry (and Lisa and Jane are across from us) with a portfolio on "Human Sexuality for the Retarded" on my lap. We are looking at pictures of male and female differences and of the female organs involved in delivering a baby. **Terry:** "I want a baby of my own when I am a little older," and added: I thought I was pregnant but I am not. I ask her again whether she knows how one gets pregnant. **Terry:** When you make love? and pointed to a picture where a man and woman are kissing. I explain that one does not get pregnant that way and take out the picture of a woman and man engaged in intercourse. **Terry:** "But, I don't want to do that! Is that nice?" I reply that it can be very nice if both want to do that, and that is the only way one can get pregnant. **Terry:** "I don't want a baby! I don't want one!" **Author:** You just mentioned you wanted a baby of your own . . . **Terry:** But I changed my mind . . . **Author:** Is that because this (pointing to the picture) has to happen first? **Terry:** Yes . . . . I want a baby. And then she points to Kitty who had entered the room in the meantime: "She has a baby. She has done that!" Kitty laughs but does not say anything. **Terry:** (Suddenly and again with interest, halfway kiddingly) "That is not fair. She did it and I haven't!" (November 6, visit 64)

Terry appeared to be the only subject who did not have the facts about intercourse and conception straight. According to the residence coordinator, all subjects had seen pictures on sexuality somewhere along their school career. Using a portfolio on sexuality, I checked with Lisa and Jane, who both stated that they knew what intercourse meant. Bob and Max mentioned that "they knew all about it." I did not directly check with Don or Pam, but the houseparent of the male cottage who did discuss issues about sexuality with the men stated that the men certainly knew.

The explicit mentioning of sexual intercourse was a very private matter. Of the eight observations that explicitly mention intercourse, six were elicited by me and two were made when I was alone with the subject. The two self-initiated comments came from Max (example 45) and Rob.

EXAMPLE 45: When talking alone with Max about his future plans, he mentioned marriage to Terry. **Max:** "I have never had it with anyone." **Author:** You mean that you have never made love with anyone? **Max:** "Yes, never." **Author:** Is that good or bad for you? **Max:** "Good, because that is not love." A little later in the conversation he repeated the same statement. (June 5, visit 7)

Three common elements in the activities noted in the observations discussed so far are (1) their forbidden nature before marriage and the negative evaluation if one would engage in them anyway, (2) the private nature about their communication, and (3) the excitement and tension of their anticipation as well as the use of their reference by the subjects as a tease and a challenge.

As noted earlier, the above is not to say that these persons would not engage in more intimate sexual behaviors if the behavioral setting were different, allowing them to be sexually involved or offering opportunities to do so anyway. The following example suggests that at least two of them might.

EXAMPLE 46: I entered the men's cottage; only Rob was home. He was cleaning the coffee pot in the kitchen and the radio played loudly. He said that he did not mind being home alone, adding: "I like it sometimes." I asked what he liked about it. **Rob:** "No one yells at me," and a little later he said: "I have sneaky plans too" (looking up at me from the corner of his eyes). **Author:** what kind of sneaky plans? **Rob:** Have a girl here . . . oh, no, I am kidding . . . He then asked what my children were doing at home. I told him they were spending the night at a friend's house. **Rob:** So you have the house for you alone? **Author:** Not quite, I have a student living in the basement. **Rob:** "I wished I lived in that basement." **Author:** Why is that? **Rob:** Well, I could have a lot of chicks there. **Author:** What would you do? **Rob:** Be fresh with them. **Author:** And what is fresh? **Rob:** Rob did not give a clear answer but instead told me a story about Don who was fresh because he had talked "crazy" about a girl he wanted to have a baby with. (November 5, visit 63)

Lighter degrees of physical/sexual involvement

So far, the observations described have referred to greater degrees of physical/sexual intimacies and to intercourse. The next observations to be discussed were coded under the properties "Lengthier Touching," "Lengthier Fooling Around," "Kissing," and "Reactions to Partial Nudity" (see Fig. 7). The main meaning that runs through all observations coded under these properties is one of fun and excitement (Examples 47 through 51).

EXAMPLE 47: Terry and I are leafing through a *Vogue* magazine that the houseparent left on the kitchen table. **Terry:** (Pointing at a man and woman embracing each other in an advertisement): "Hobby, hobby!" I ask what that word means. **Terry:** "Ask Lisa." **Lisa:** Oh, you say that when you see something beautiful, or exciting, or pretty. Terry sees a woman in a bra and says "hobby, hobby" again. (September 1, visit 48)

EXAMPLE 48: We were driving back from a hayride, Kitty and Rob laying in the back, fooling around, tickling, teasing, pushing, and laughing. Before going to the cottages, the recreation worker went to a supermarket to buy something. We all waited in the car. Rob was saying something to Kitty. **Kitty:** (Laughing) "He is saying something about sexy girls." A little later Rob intensely watched a girl passing by wearing a halter top, and said to himself: "Hey, you, sexy thing!" (July 5, visit 19).

EXAMPLE 49: Lisa had picked up the portfolio on "Human Sexuality for the Retarded." We were sitting in the living room, talking. She took out a picture of the female genitals (a woman in delivery position) and giggled, showing it to Terry and Kitty on the couch across from us. They said giggling: "Shame, Lisa, shame!" (November 6, visit 64)

EXAMPLE 50: In the car, on our way to the public library, Rob and Kitty talked about the film they went to see the night before. I asked how they liked it. Kitty said it was funny. All Rob said was that there was a naked woman . . . and he added: "I liked it, liked it . . . I loved it!" **Author:** But what was the story about? **Rob:** "A naked woman." **Author:** What happened to her? No answer. (July 26, visit 29)

EXAMPLE 51: On television the Sunday afternoon movie featured Elvis Presley. A strip dancer was performing in a nightclub. **Lisa:** "Oh, I hope that Jimmie (her boyfriend) is not watching this," and added: I told him he can't watch those things. **Author:** Why is that? **Lisa:** "Well . . ." **Author:** What happens when he watches it? **Lisa:** "Well, you know . . ." **Author:** So, you don't want him to watch. **Lisa:** No, but he says I am not his boss, so . . . **Author:** But why can't he though? Lisa shrugs her shoulders. **Author:** Would you be jealous? **Lisa:** "Yes, very . . . she is too pretty!" (November 6, visit 64)

All acts contained in the field notes and coded under the

properties "Lengthier Touching" and "Kissing" took place in established boy/girl friend relationships. Acts coded under "Lengthier Fooling Around" also occurred between the sexes outside of the boy/girl friend relationships. For instance, Rob and Terry, who were not in a boy/girl friend relationship, did fool around on many occasions. Likewise, these behaviors went on between Kitty and Rob and between Kitty and another workshop client.*

> EXAMPLE 52: I went over to the women's cottage where the television was on. Lisa, Jane, Kitty, and Terry were sitting around and Rob was visiting. He was sitting next to Terry, close to her, his arm around her shoulder. They were joking for the next ten minutes and fooling around. They tickled each other, punched and pushed. (June 22, visit 14)

> EXAMPLE 53: Jane had sat down with her boyfriend on the other side of the corridor, very close, and they were caressing each other, seemingly oblivious to the world. (August 16, visit 43)

The behaviors coded under lighter degrees of physical/sexual involvement differ from those indicating more intimate degrees in several ways: (1) they are not explicitly characterized as forbidden; (2) nowhere is marriage mentioned as needed for involvement; (3) they are accessible (except at work), and (4) they can be referred to and engaged in group settings.

The similarity between these two clusters of data is to be found in the mixture of meanings of anticipation, fun, excitement, and tension, and in their use as a tease and/or challenge. This mixture of meanings runs through all data from which this pattern emerged.

Before discussing some negative cases, some additional comments about the data of this pattern may be of interest. First, the behaviors in sixty-six of the seventy-seven observations relevant to the discussion so far were triggered by a stimulus that contained a

---

*The word "client" in this study refers to an employee at the workshop who lived in the community, rather than in the group home.

clearly observable physical/sexual element: something they saw on television or in the movies, a girl passing by, a book, a rumor of pregnancy, a question I asked, a remark by a staff member. Only eight observations reflected self-initiated comments with no clearly observable stimulus. Two examples are offered.

> EXAMPLE 54: After recreation, we all walk back from the workshop building to the cottages. I walk next to Jane and Rob. Kitty and Terry are in front of us. Kitty turns her head and says to me: "I got in trouble today, but I won't tell why!" Rob teases her and I catch the words "Hanky panky." Kitty reacts: "Rob! No!" and laughingly pushes him away. (September 20, visit 52)

> EXAMPLE 55: We are in my car driving back from an outing in town. **Kitty:** Sandy (recreation worker) said that there would be a surprise for us. **Volunteer:** Lous and I know what it is but we are not going to say. **Author:** All I know is that I have orders to go back. **Rob:** I bet it is a beer party or so. **Kitty:** "Beer!" Not on my backdoor!" **Rob:** "Or a party where men and women are doing hanky panky stuff!" **Kitty:** "Rob! Not with you! not on my backdoor!" A lot of laughter with all that. (July 26, visit 29)

Second, it seems safe to state that the overriding meaning of physical/sexual intimacies and the projected meaning of intercourse is one of desirability of these intimacies for their own sake and not one connected with the desire to have children. Lisa seemed to sum this up in a very concentrated way.

> EXAMPLE 56: **Author:** Would you want to have a child after you were married? **Lisa:** "Yes, a boy. I want a boy." **Author:** Why is that? **Lisa:** "Well, . . . you know . . . a boy can't get pregnant! And also, he does not have these monthly things . . . you know." (January 5, visit 77)

Here, Lisa surely viewed sexual behavior apart from its reproductive function, and such a view seems very representative of the majority of the subjects.

Third, many times, marriage was referred to in a teasing context. In twenty observations subjects teased each other with the idea of marriage, as shown in the following examples.

> Example 57: After a visit to the home of one of the recreation workers, we are waiting outside for Jane, who can't be found. Kitty and Teresa and another female client are teasing each other, calling each other "Mrs. ——— (name of boyfriend) and pushing and laughing. (September 6, visit 46)

> Example 58: Kitty talks again about a book on marriage in the public library that she had wanted to check out. **Rob:** "Who are you going to marry?" **Kitty:** "Not you!" Rob: "Marry a dog . . . a horse." They then go into a whole nonsense talk of who Kitty can marry. (July 26, visit 29)

These observations raise the question: Why do these persons tease each other with the concept of marriage? The data may imply a relation between the element of tease and challenge running through many observations from which the pattern on physical/sexual involvement emerged, and the use of the concept of marriage as a teasing device. Since the subjects saw marriage and sexual involvement as almost interchangeable, and since sexual involvement contained strong elements of tease and challenge, the use of the concept of marriage as a teasing device may be related to the marriage-sex connection.

A search for negative cases, with regard to all aspects of this pattern, did not render many observations. In fact, only one explicit negative case could be found. Pam, in the following observation, negated the exciting element in partial nudity:

> Example 59: When visiting at my house, Jane who was leafing through magazines, showed a picture of a woman taking a shower (advertisement) to others around her, while giggling much about it. Others (Lisa, Kitty, Terry, Rob) started giggling, too, and laughing, saying: "Oh, oh." Then the volunteer who was also present said

> that it was nothing abnormal. **Lisa:** That is natural; that is just natural. **Pam:** That is just a body. Why laugh about it? (October 25, visit 58)

Looking across all subjects and their contribution to the data from which this pattern emerged, five persons of the eight contributed substantially to all properties involved. Kitty, Pam, and Don contributed to some but not to others. Kitty never expressed herself about the meanings of intercourse and higher levels of sexual involvement, but contributed greatly to all other properties. In contrast, Don and Pam did not contribute at all to the observations on lighter degrees of physical intimacies, though Pam did respond to my questions on the marriage-sex connection.

For Kitty there seems to be no other explanation than the one given before, namely her deviant background. Marriage and related issues were clearly not desirable for her at this point in her life. However, involvement in and commenting on lighter degrees of physical intimacies and partial nudity did appeal to her as well as some "fooling around" outside of the more established boy/girl friend relationships.

While Don contributed little to my direct observations, the field notes contain relevant background information about him from staff members as well as from Rob. These notes indicate his quarrels with Rob about a girl friend in the workshop. Also, according to Rob, Don at times talks "silly" and "stupid" about the issues of girls and sex:

> EXAMPLE 60: Alone with Rob, he told me about Don who had been "fresh." He had wanted the phone number of a girl whom Rob had told him about (from Rob's church). Don had said something about calling her and having a baby and taking her to the hospital to have a baby and buying diapers. That kind of talk was "fresh" and "crazy" according to Rob. (November 5, visit 63)

Thus, Kitty, Don, and Pam were unrepresentative for some properties from which this pattern emerged, but not for others. They were unrepresentative by partial absence rather than by explicit negative statements. All three did engage in some of the behaviors. It may well be their particular personalities and backgrounds that prevented them from exhibiting all relevant behaviors openly.

It also needs to be kept in mind that the data presented in this pattern must only represent a part of the subjects' construction of their sexuality, that part they felt comfortable showing in my presence.

In all, the pattern of Marriage and Physical/Sexual Involvement seemed to be an important and a stable one for the persons of this study.

Discussion

Stereotypes regarding sexuality of the retarded have run the entire gamut of "sexless and infertile" to "oversexed and perverted" (Edgerton, 1967, p. 112). Until recent years, very few facts were known (Edgerton, 1967; Gordon, 1971). Recently, research has illuminated this neglected area. Consistently, these studies report that none of the stereotypes are accurate, that sexual development in persons labeled retarded is clearly present, and that this development broadly follows the same growth pattern as that for unlabeled persons (Deisher, 1973; Edgerton, 1967, 1973; Gordon, 1973; Johnson, 1973; Morgenstern, 1973).

Edgerton (1973) elaborates on the problem of definition when attempting research on "sexuality and the retarded." He raises the questions: What do we mean by "sexual" behavior and what do we mean by "the retarded?" By sexual, Edgerton (1973, p. 242) states: ". . . we must mean more than the expression of genital sexuality, for that is an absurdly narrow definition." Furthermore, as the concept "mentally retarded" embraces an almost limitless heterogeneity, we must specify which mentally retarded we mean. The second problem is to learn how the persons labeled retarded construe *their* sexual domain: "It is one thing to define sexual behavior as we wish to study it and quite another thing to define it as the subjects in our study do" (Edgerton, 1973, p. 243).

The findings in this pattern of the present study illustrate the importance of Edgerton's comments. While the subjects never used the words sex or sexuality, they provided definitions in terms of the meanings they attached to different levels of physical contact. These distinct meanings were influenced by the following conditions: (1) whether or not one was married: this could change the same meaning of the behavior into love or not love; (2) whether or not one was in a boy/girl relationship: this would make the behavior allowable and an expression of fun and/or affection, or not allowable; (3) when not being in a boy/girl friend relationship, certain behaviors could still be engaged in, but they acquired the meaning of fun, challenge, and a "try-out" gesture; (4) whether or not one was in a group setting as opposed to a one-to-one serious conversation: this made discussing matters of physical contact either jokingly light or serious. Thus, for these persons, living in a strictly supervised group home setting where anything beyond lighter degrees of physical contact was not allowed and where little serious talk about sexual matters occurred, the conditions of marriage, of being or not being in a boy/girl friend relationship, of being in a group setting or in a one-to-one serious conversation, were decisive factors in the way they construed their sexuality.

A review of the literature did not show the conservative marriage-sex connection as expressed by the subjects of this study. On the contrary, Johnson (1973, p. 59) speculates: ". . . It (sex) may well have little or nothing to do with establishing or maintaining a permanent or even long term relationship, and it does not necessarily occur with love or marriage." Brantlinger (personal communication) finds that the connection between marriage and sex does not exist in the total institution where she carried out her research (Brantlinger, 1978). Sex is something "they just do."

In this group-home setting, where the supervision was very close (as it was in the workshop) and where there was always at least one staff member present (and often more), opportunities for unacceptable sexual involvement were hard to create. In addition, the possibility of "getting out of here" depended upon subjects' correct behavior, of which abstinence of sexual involvement was a major ingredient.

Hilbert (1977) notes a major theme of the ethnomethodological viewpoint: in order to make sense of the world, members must rely upon their assumption that reality is noncontradictory in nature. It seems highly likely that the subjects of this study made the marriage-sex connection to make their reality noncontradictory. As Rob stated: "I have a new girl friend, but I am not going to bed with her. I am not ready yet and I am not married." (November 15, visit 68).

Another point to be noted is the fact that these persons, while being sexual as are the rest of us, having their minds on sexual matters and expressing a great interest, need, and desire for physical/sexual contact with a person of the opposite sex, can abstain from engagement in heterosexual behavior. Edgerton (1973) concludes from his research that the mildly retarded are capable of truly remarkable sexual self-control. To my knowledge, Edgerton is the only one who has pointed out this fact in the face of the assumption (which pervades our professional literature as well as common belief) that the less competent are less capable than the rest of us of controlling sexual impulses (hence, the need for close supervision, confinement, sterilization, and the like). The subjects of the present study, clearly, could wait. There is enough evidence that their ability to abstain from higher degrees of heterosexual involvement is not caused by being sexless. Alleviating this contradiction in their lives by using the marriage-sex connection as a rationalization apparently worked for them and allowed them to view their reality as orderly. Nevertheless, their ability to abstain from heterosexual activity for many years during their adult lives, while so much in their surroundings stimulated its preoccupation, is indeed remarkable in the face of extant stereotypes.

While heterosexual activity was very limited, homosexual involvement and masturbation did occur, according to information obtained from houseparents. I have no data that directly reflect the ways the subjects gave meaning to these expressions of sexuality. It would have been one of several other aspects of their lives worthy of inquiry; however, such was not feasible within the scope of this study.

In sum, the findings of this pattern show the oversimplification of general comments about "sexuality and the retarded." The data emphasize the complexity we have to deal with if we want to understand how persons we have labeled retarded, in their specific environments, construe their sexuality.

Attitudes by community, parents, and staff members and administrators of institutions with regard to sexuality for "the retarded" have been found to be very conservative as compared to attitudes on sexuality for the general population. These attitudes reflect that persons labeled retarded are thought of in stereotypic ways and are not allowed to make their own sexual decisions (Brantlinger, 1978; Deisher, 1973; Morgenstern, 1973). This belief system was certainly true for the group-home setting of the present study, where (1) no sexual involvement beyond lighter degrees of physical contact (holding hands, sitting close) was allowed for the eighteen to forty year old subjects, (2) no privacy was allowed with regard to being with a member of the opposite sex, and (3) no sex education or serious conversations about sexuality was systematically provided; sex education and communication about sexual matters seemed to be shunned in almost all cases. Noting these facts is not an evaluative remark, but an illustration that the general state-of-the-art was also true for the setting of this study. As Gordon (1971) notes: the topic of sex is missing in special education.

Absence of sex education and open communication about sexual matters has been consistently noted (Edgerton, 1967; Garuth, 1973; Gordon, 1971, 1977). Says one of Edgerton's (1967, p. 31) subjects: "That hospital sure didn't teach nothing about marriage life . . . They sure don't teach you about the bees and the . . ." (the person could not remember what went with the bees in the phrase). The literature since does not reflect much improvement. Gordon (1977, p. 9) comments on this state of affairs as follows: "I think it is immoral for institutions and parents not to provide mentally retarded people in their charge with sex education . . ." It would seem that one reason why marriage has not been considered as an alternative in the systematic planning and programming of rehabilitation programs may lay in our belief system of sexuality in general and for "the retarded" in particular.

Edgerton (1973) comments that exposure to community living, where sexual behavior and attitudes are rapidly changing, increases the need for open communication about sexuality. The findings of the present study exemplify the urgency of this statement. Subjects were constantly exposed to sexual matters in some form or other, such as films, television, pictures in magazines, popular songs, observing people in the community, and even comments (though perhaps made quite unconsciously) by some staff members, as is shown in the following examples:

> **Recreation worker:** "I am sleepy," and to Don, as he walks out of the door (in a challenging tone): "I sleep with you tonight!" (July 3, visit 18)
>
> We arrive at the workshop to go downtown to the public library. A recreation worker says to Bob (a resident, but not one of the subjects), whose shirt was unbuttoned: "Do you look sexy with that hairy chest sticking out!" (June 2, visit 7)

It must be stressed that such remarks only came from a few staff members and certainly were not typical for the staff in general. Nevertheless, the point is that much of the subjects' day to day exposure was colored by reference to sexual matters. As was noted in the discussion of this pattern, most of the behaviors from which the pattern emerged were responses to the kind of stimuli referred to above.

That researchers are not free from these influences, and also consciously ignore matters of sexuality, is patently reflected in the writings by Henshel (1972) and Mattinson (1970, 1973). While both researchers focused on marriage and children, the topic of sexuality and the subjects' perceptions thereof are conspiciously absent. Henshel (1972, p. 8) states:

> It will be noted that sex (attitudes toward, frequency of coitus, positions used), a matter of great emphasis in current psychological and sociological literature, was not discussed. While such information would certainly have been intriguing, it was not necessary in order to realize the goals of this study. The decision to eliminate this issue was influenced by other considerations. First, the respondents were told that we wanted to know about their work and their general situation, and legitimizing questions about sex would thus have been difficult, especially since several of our other inquiries — such as those covering the gamut of marital involvement — were also tenuously justifiable. Second, sex is a perilous topic, needless to say, and the individuals might have felt that we were prying unnecessarily into their lives had this sanctum been entered. Third, some might have mentioned to others, such as parents and counselors, that we were asking

them 'indecent' questions, and the resultant uproar can be easily imagined, as outsiders might have felt that we were exploiting these persons because of their vulnerability. All such reactions are understandable, and we therefore shied away from The Topic.

Given this attitude it is hardly surprising that we know so little of the ways the less competent in our care give meaning to their sexuality. Unfortunately, ignorance, fear, and reluctance to open our eyes continue to leave space for stereotypes and attitudes that are inconsistent with reality, and that may well block serious consideration of marriage as an alternative life-style. While independent living for certain aspects of life is encouraged and facilitated in line with normalization and deinstitutionalization principles, marriage is not. Given that marriage may be a viable and positive proposition for some of the less competent who desire married life—as most of the subjects of this study—it would be unfortunate indeed if our belief system on sexuality would hinder facilitation of marriage. To quote Money (1973, p. 11), a noted American sexuologist: "Only if one can be completely nonjudgmental about sex can one think clearly about the wisdom and possibility of making proper arrangements for conjugal living where mentally retarded members of the two sexes can become true partners."

MARRIAGE AND CHILDREN

This small but interesting pattern shows the subjects' taken-for-granted notion that, since having children goes with being married, and since marriage is a possibility, having children is a possibility.

Two properties contributed to this pattern (Fig. 8).

Most subjects simply assumed they would have children once married. Not much thought was given to this assumption. Table V shows a total of eighteen observations for this pattern. Sixteen of these eighteen observations were elicited; in only two was a desire for children volunteered. The latter was the case in Example 61:

EXAMPLE 61: **Rob:** "I'll be married and happy. Being single . . ." **Author:** But you live with a group of other

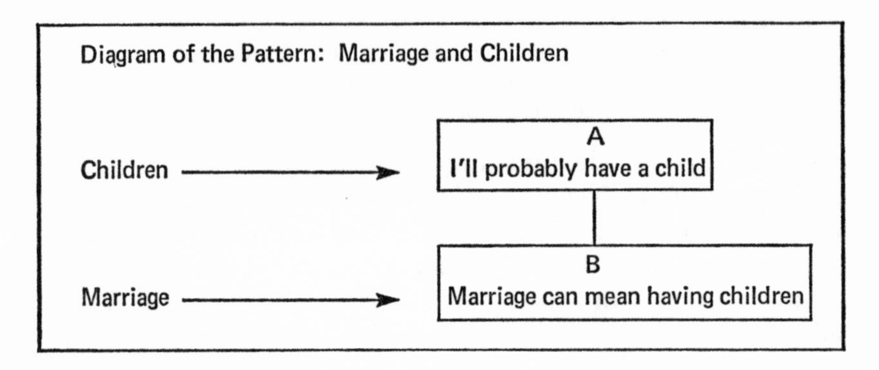

DEFINITIONS

Category: Children: Any act or verbal statement reflecting a meaning the subjects gave to having and rearing children.

Property A: Having children is seen as a possibility. One sees oneself capable of having and rearing children, if not now, then at some point in the future.

Category: Marriage: Any act or verbal statement reflecting a meaning the subjects gave to married life.

Property B: Marriage means the possibility of having children.

Figure 8.

Table V

Frequencies of Observations of the Pattern: Marriage and Children

Properties	*Volunteered*	*Elicited*	*Total*
I'll probably have a child	1	9	10
Marriage can mean having children	1	7	8
Total	2	16	18

people, don't you? **Rob:** "Yes, but I want a family, children of my own, you know . . . raise my own children . . . the right way." **Author:** You want children . . . how many would you want? **Rob:** "Two." **Author:** Children are quite something to have. **Rob:** Oh, yes. **Author:** A lot of energy, time, and money. But they are also very nice to have around. **Rob:** I want maybe four, two girls and two boys. (May 23, visit 2)

The second voluntary comment indicating a desire for children came from Terry, who mentioned that she wanted "a baby of my own when I am a little older." While Rob's remark was within the context of a conversation about marriage, Terry's comment was made during a conversation on the biological aspects of having a baby. It may be noted that even Rob's desire to have children of his own seemed secondary to his desire to be married, as a subsequent part of our conversation indicates:

EXAMPLE 62: **Author:** So, you want children. What if your wife would not want children for whatever reason? **Rob:** I would not hassle her. Till she would be ready. **Author:** She might just not want them and, therefore, never be ready. How would you feel about that? **Rob:** That would be OK. (May 23, visit 2)

There were three more elicited comments expressing a desire to have a child. I asked: Would you want a child? The responses follow:

Lisa: "Yes, a boy . . . I want a boy." (January 5, visit 77)

Pam: "Yes, but not yet. I have enough to do with myself" (laughing as she said so). (August 10, visit 35)

Max: Yes, two, if Terry can handle it. I would not even be afraid of adopting children. (June 5, visit 7)

The remaining thirteen observations simply reflected the notion: Yes, I'll probably have a child.

Having and rearing a child, then, appeared to be a rather abstract notion. While subjects gave a variety of meanings to the concept of marriage that related to their present actual needs, having a child was not invested with much meaning. Apparently, at this point in their lives and in the particular behavioral setting, these persons experienced few needs that gave rise to the projection of having children.

A search for negative cases rendered few observations. Two of them came from Terry. One of her negative expressions came after the discovery that in order to have a baby she would have to have sexual intercourse (example 44). The other negative comment was made under the influence of a significant other:

> EXAMPLE 63: In my car, on the way to a concert, Terry talked about the possibility of marrying her present boyfriend. **Terry:** I would not have children . . . not for a while. **Author:** You told me the other day that you would want a child . . . have you changed your mind? **Terry:** Yes, but my mam (foster mother) says that I better not . . . can't do things together. "It is no fun when you have to take care of a baby." (November 9, visit 65)

A negative case came from Kitty who conceded the possibility of marriage but said "No" to having another child (January 5, visit 77). It is interesting to note that Kitty twice volunteered a comment about her own child:

> EXAMPLE 64: **Kitty:** (Spontaneously) "Carl (her child) has had his birthday; he is three now. Ms. ——— (social worker) said he is in ——— (location) but that is far. I have not seen him for a long time now." (July 3, visit 18)

On another occasion (see example 5) Kitty stated that she would have her child back when she would have a place of her own. After not having seen her child for years, she clearly considered him still her own and had hopes of getting him back. Given Kitty's background, it is easy to speculate why she did not want to have another child, and her reasons would not seem representative for the population under study.

Another negative case comes from Jane, who, also under the influence of a significant other, stated that she might not be capable of taking care of a baby. She mentioned that she could not marry because her mam had said so (since she "can't cook good things and can't read and write" see Example 20).

> EXAMPLE 65: **Jane:** "And I can't take care of a baby." **Author:** How do you know, Jane? **Jane:** "My mom says that." **Author:** But do *you* want a child — do you think you could take care of it? **Jane:** (Nodding yes) "Yeah

> . . . I think so." (January 5, visit 77)
>
> EXAMPLE 66: On another occasion, Kitty and Terry were teasing each other by calling each other "Mrs." and then the name of their respective boyfriends. They said to Jane: And you are Mrs. Johnson (name of Jane's boyfriend)? **Jane:** "I am not Mrs. Johnson, I can't marry." **Author:** Why is that, Jane? **Jane:** "Well . . . I can't read, can't write. I can't . . . (could not understand her)." **Lisa:** "With whom have you been?" **Jane:** "With my grandmom." **Lisa:** "Oh . . . (with the intonation: that is where it comes from)." **Jane:** "My grandmom says that I can't marry as I can't do reading and writing." **Houseparent:** "Well, Bill can still be a good friend even if you don't marry him." (September 9, visit 48)

It is doubtful whether this observation should be considered a truly negative case. It would clearly depend on the strength of the influence exerted by Jane's relatives when the actuality of marriage and children came about. Jane, in this case, was clearly not happy with her mother's opinion, as was reflected in her intonation and in the reactions by the other subjects and houseparent. They all conveyed a consoling and "don't let someone else tell you" attitude.

In Kitty's and Terry's cases, significant others have not succeeded in influencing them to think of themselves as not capable of having and rearing children. Kitty clearly hopes to have her own child back again. Terry considers having a child as a possibility, regardless of the attempts by the resident coordinator and the director of the workshop to obtain her consent for sterilization, while attempting to convince her that she is not capable of rearing children.

In sum, having children was not a particularly important issue at this point in the subjects' lives. However, its importance may lie in the almost automatic assumption that, once married, having children would be part of their lives.

Discussion

What is the real possibility that these subjects, if they marry, would have children? Would they want children at that point?

If so, could they make adequate parents? Would it be likely that their children would be judged incompetent?

Farber (1968) notes a consistent finding that approximately 40 percent of the children are judged retarded when both parents are; when only one parent is retarded, a range of 8–20 percent of the off-spring are found to be retarded. In Mattinson's (1970) study, seventeen of the thirty-six couples (or 47%) had forty children among them. Six of these forty children (belonging to three families) had been committed to the care of local authorities. Almost half of the children were judged by their teachers as not normally adjusted. Of the twenty-three preschoolers, however, only one was evaluated retarded in general development. None of these twenty-three preschoolers appeared malnourished or unfairly treated.

In Henshel's (1972) study, twenty-four of the couples had become parents. They totaled sixty-six children, of whom two had been taken away to be placed under local authority. Fifteen (or 23%) of these sixty-six children were judged to be handicapped. In terms of adequacy in parenting, Henshel comments on the parents' amazing tolerance of their children's handicaps and retardation, of which they were well aware. Researchers found both erratic and consistent patterns of child rearing, but, in all, parents seemed loving. Many of the children were judged hyperactive.

All but two of Edgerton's subjects had been sterilized before discharge from the hospital. These two subjects, both women, had children and were "markedly successful" in raising them (Edgerton, 1967, p. 124). Nevertheless, Edgerton (1973) expresses his doubts about the adequacy of parental skills of less competent persons, especially in the light of typical poor economic circumstances and possible genetic influences. For similar reasons, Wolfensberger (1972), stimulated by his exposure to Scandinavian conceptualization of normalization principles, which matter of factly included sex and marriage, is an advocate of a childless marriage for most of the mildly retarded as well as for the severely retarded and impaired. A very outspoken opinion is voiced by Gordon (1977). He considers it unacceptable and cruel when persons who cannot take care of themselves are consciously or covertly encouraged to have children.

Clearly, the judgment of adequacy is a relative one at best. It may also be a rather arrogant one. As both Edgerton (1973) and Wolfensberger (1972) note, few normal persons make adequate parents. Nevertheless, the burden of child rearing seems particularly heavy for the less competent.

The relation between these findings and the findings of this pattern lies in the possibility that having children may become very important once married. Especially for most of the women in the studies by Edgerton (1967), Henshel (1972), and Mattinson (1970), having children was of great importance to their self-esteem. For the couple described by Meyers (1978), having children was seen as crucial to their self-esteem, especially for the husband. After they married, the couple badly wanted children. Stated the husband: "That's what regular people do. They get married and have children and a house. That's what we wanted too." (Meyers, 1978, p. 107).

While having children was very important for Edgerton's (1967) subjects, especially for the women, it is not clear to what extent their desire to have children was a reaction to their mandatory sterilization, which they typically wanted to hide from their lovers and husbands. Henshel (1972) found that three female subjects were enthusiastic about the possibility of sterilization, and five women who were pregnant during the time of the research resented it.

In sum, no definite conclusion about the desirability of having children by persons we label retarded seems warranted. While it is known that marriage may be a viable and beneficial alternative, and while having children seems to be a matter-of-fact event to the unmarried, it is not clear that having children is necessarily crucial to their self-esteem. Moreover, the evidence seems to indicate that having children is often too great a burden for the less competent. Nevertheless, it should be considered, with regard to the planning and implementation of rehabilitation programs, that having children may become very important once these persons marry. In the summary chapter, these issues will be addressed once more in an attempt to outline thoughts for further research and program planning.

MARRIAGE AND BOY/GIRL FRIEND RELATIONSHIPS

When analyzing the data, it became clear that the meanings the subjects gave to boy/girl friend relationships had as much to do (if not more) with their projection of marriage as with meanings relative to concrete day-to-day needs. It therefore seemed appropriate to discuss this pattern in relation to the subjects' views on marriage. The diagram of this pattern is depicted in Figure 9.

To have or not to have—it seemed of great importance to all subjects but one. Even that one, Kitty, had a boyfriend according to others:

> EXAMPLE 67: Kitty and Terry are talking about Jo-Ann (a client at the workshop) and calling her a "trouble maker." **Author:** Why is she a trouble maker? **Terry:** Oh, she tries to take all our boyfriends away. She tries to be with Max all the time . . . and she does the same with Kitty. **Author:** Who is Kitty's boyfriend? **Terry:** Dave . . . and Jo-Ann also tries to take him away from Kitty. (September 6, visit 46)

The field notes reflect several observations of Kitty with Dave, spending the breaktimes together and fooling around. However, Kitty herself shied away from the acknowledgement of having a boyfriend. Likewise, she resisted the idea of dating:

> EXAMPLE 68: On the Sunday afternoon movie, Elvis Presley is taking a ten-year-old girl out in his helicopter and starts singing a song to her. It contains the sentence: ". . . you'll be dating too." **Kitty:** "He says dating . . . you hear that?" She looks at all of us. **Author:** Wouldn't you want to date? **Kitty:** "I? No!" **Author:** Why is is that? **Kitty:** Smiled and shrugged her shoulders. (November 15, visit 68)

At the outset of the description of the pattern, the one unrepresentative case has thus been stated. However, given Kitty's somewhat steady male companion at work with whom she did "fool around" and her reactions to issues about boyfriends as reflected in example 68, it is safe to say that she was not just indifferent and uninterested.

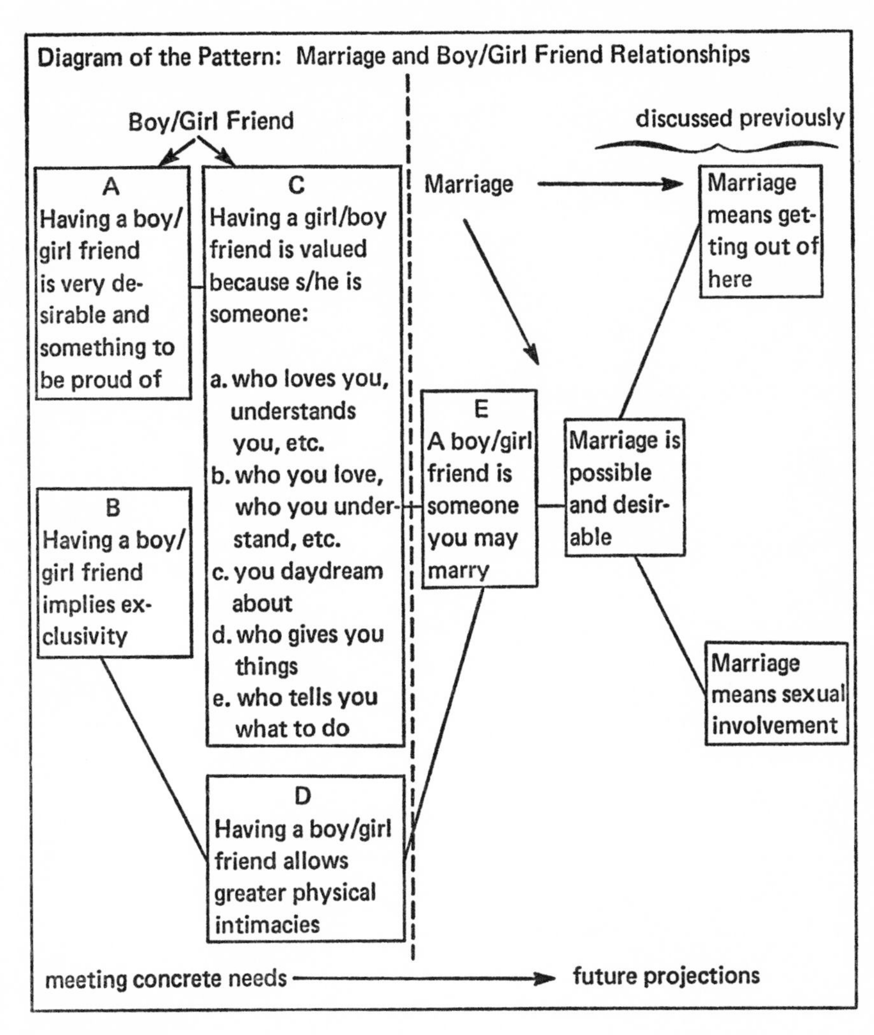

DEFINITIONS

Category: Boy/Girl Friend: Any act or verbal statement reflecting a meaning the subjects gave to boy/girl friend relationships.

Property A: Having a boy/girl friend is desirable, and, if one has one, it is something to be proud of and to tell others about.

B: Having a boy/girl friend means belonging to each other, waiting for each other, being jealous about each other, or fighting for each other (notion of exclusivity and possessiveness).

Figure 9.

C: a. A boy/girl friend is viewed in terms of one's own needs: s/he is someone you need, whom you miss, who understands you, who loves you, or who is concerned about you.

b. A boy/girl friend is viewed in terms of the other: S/he is someone whom you are concerned about, whom you love, whom you try to understand, who misses you, or who needs you.

c. A boy/girl friend is someone you daydream about.

d. A boy/girl friend is someone whose bond with you is expressed in gifts.

e. A boy/girl friend is someone who gives you guidelines for behavior or acts as an authority figure.

D: A boy/girl friend is someone whom you can kiss and be more physically intimate with.

E: A boy/girl friend is someone whom you may marry.

Table VI
Frequency Distribution of Observations of the Pattern:
Marriage and Boy/Girl Friend Relationships

Properties	*Volunteered*	*Elicited*	*Total*
A. Having a boy/girl friend is very desirable and something to be proud of	16	6	22
B. Having a boy/girl friend implies exclusivity	17	7	24
	33	13	46
C. Having a girl/boy friend is valued because s/he is someone:			
a. who loves you, understands you, etc.	4	4	8
b. who you love, who you understand, etc.	10	—	10
c. you daydream about	2	3	5
d. who gives you things	8	1	9
e. who tells you what to do	4	1	5
	28	9	37
D. Having a boy/girl friend allows for greater physical intimacy (17 acts)	5	6	28
E. A boy/girl friend is someone you may marry	12	4	16
Total	79	31	127

The property "having a boy/girl friend is very desirable and something to be proud of" (Property A) contained twenty-two observations. This number is very conservative as it only includes observations that reflect the notion: I am proud or glad to have a boy/girl friend, or, I would like to have one. Over sixty other observations express the following reasons why having a boy/girl friend is desirable: for being loved and cared for, for companionship, to dream about, to be physically intimate with, to talk with, to marry, to get presents from, and from whom to receive guidelines for behavior.

> Example 69: As we are driving on third street on our way to Lake Monroe, Lisa, sitting next to me, suddenly claps her hands excitedly and says: That was my boyfriend. He is a cuty! (June 11, visit 11)
>
> Example 70: Just before we all went over to the workshop to go to recreation, the recreation worker introduced a new volunteer. She mentioned everyone's name to the new person. After that, Terry went to the new volunteer and said: "Max my boyfriend is not coming. He is my boyfriend." (July 10, visit 28)
>
> Example 71: Max and I were sitting in front of the men's cottage on the little wall, talking. He told me about a girl friend in the hospital where he had spent three years, whom he had loved very much and wanted to marry. However, his mother had not allowed him to. He added: "That's why I hate my mother." He then said: I wished I had a picture of her (girl friend). She was with me all the time. (August 20, visit 37)
>
> Example 72: I had gone to the men's cottage to see what went on. No one was there but Rob. He walked with me outside and said that he had been dreaming. **Author:** About what? **Rob:** (Laughing) About sexy girls. And a little later: Well, I have a new girfriend now, but I don't go to bed with her. I am not ready for that yet. (November 16, visit 69)
>
> Example 73: When talking to Pam, on the way back from a concert in town, she mentioned that there was no

one at the workshop she was interested in dating, but that she would like to date a certain supervisor. (October 26, visit 59)

EXAMPLE 74: Lisa, Terry, Jane, and myself are talking in the living room. The conversation came to Max, who had been taken back to an institution. Lisa told us how, when she saw him the first time, she had thought, "Who is that good-looking blond there?" **Terry:** "I don't like the name Heking (Max's last name); I like Johnson (name of current boyfriend) better, and I hate Nelson" (her own last name). (November 15, visit 68)

The last example strikingly shows the projecting of oneself onto a boyfriend. Boy/girl friends were indeed a frequent topic of conversation. The only one not interested in such conversations was Pam, who complained to me that the other women always talked about boys: ". . . always about boys . . . and then they need a shoulder to cry on" (example 7). Jane, however, expressed how the topic was a vital one to keep their many conversations alive:

EXAMPLE 75: I am talking with Lisa and Jane in the living room. They mention that the weekend houseparent does not allow them to talk about families or boyfriends. They can't talk about their families because it would make them sad. **Jane:** "And we can't talk about boys, either. We can't talk about nothing." **Lisa:** We can talk about work and . . . **Jane:** (Interrupts) "That's no fun, talking about work!" (January 19, visit 79)

The topic is a vital one indeed given the many conversations, discussions, arguments about boy/girl friends, and actual acts of being together with a boy/girl friend.

During the period of the research, boy/girl friend relations were carried out between Max and Terry and between all other subjects but Pam with their respective boy/girl friends at the workshop. Those relations were more or less stable. Some broke up because one of the partners left, as was the case with Terry and Max and with Jane and Bill. In both cases the man was placed in another situation.

In some relations the partners shifted. Such was the case with Rob, for whom it seemed vital to have a girl friend through whom he could project his strong desires for marriage and sex. Terry, after Max left, tried out a variety of boyfriends, though she continuously referred back to Max expressing her desire "to have him back," or for him "to come and get me." She would tell me rumors that Max would be coming back. None of these rumors held any truth.

Another property (Property B) reflects the need for identification through a boy/girl friend. Property B reads: "Having a boy/girl friend means belonging to each other, waiting for each other, being jealous about each other or fighting for each other" (notion of exclusivity and possessiveness).

The field notes reflect many hear-say incidents of quarrels about taking away each other's boy/girl friend, some of which even took on the proportion of a life fight. There were arguments between Rob and Don over a certain girl and a few heated discussions about incidents that happened over the issue of who belongs to whom, as illustrated by example 77. Notes on hear-say incidents typically read as illustrated in example 76. Example 78 shows that at least sometimes these arguments were solved.

> EXAMPLE 76: The houseparent told me that Rob and Don had been fighting (yelling, smashing doors) over a girl at the workshop they both claimed as a girl friend. (December 5, visit 70)
>
> EXAMPLE 77: Late Saturday morning, Lisa and Terry are watching TV, but at the same time discussing the latest happenings at work. Terry is expressing her anger at Max who had paid too much attention to Jo-Ann, a client at the workshop. **Terry:** "Jo-Ann is a troublemaker. I feel like busting her in the mouth!" And she went on: Well, if he wants to date Jo-Ann he can do that. I'll have Philip, or Wayne . . . and if he wants me he has to fight for me, doesn't he Lisa? **Lisa:** Yes, that is the way it is; then he will have to fight for you. **Terry:** And I'll fight for him if I want him. **Lisa:** "Well, you better make up

your mind who you want first before you start fighting." And she added: If you fight for Max, then you have to give him time. "Give him time. If you really want him he is worth waiting for." **Terry:** "Give him time . . . give him time. . . that is what everyone at the workshop says!" (September 9, visit 48)

EXAMPLE 78: Terry informed me, while walking from the car to the auditorium where we were going to see a circus performance, that she and Kitty were not fighting anymore. They had decided that they did not have to fight about boyfriends, as "I first belong to Max, and then to Wayne, but that does not mean that she can't be with Wayne, too. We are just friends." (July 16, visit 27)

Terry's concern about having a boyfriend is clearly expressed in the last example. All through the research, her major desire seemed to rest with Max, but she would have others for potential replacement. Lisa expressed similar desire for security in having a boyfriend by keeping a second one on hand:

EXAMPLE 79: After Lisa and I had been out to the bank and for coffee, I took her to the cottage where no one was home. We sat down for a moment and she started talking about her boyfriend Jimmie. **Lisa:** People say you can only have one boyfriend, but "I have two. Jimmie is twenty-seven. He is younger than I am, but I like the younger ones." **Author:** So you have two. How does that make you feel? **Lisa:** Good. Then I always have one, but "Jimmie is my number one boy." (January 21, visit 81)

This desire for continuity in having a boy/girl friend (which implies shifting partners when necessary) also characterized Max's, Rob's, and Don's behavior. I observed little of Don's behavior myself, due much to his shy personality, his great reserve in speaking about these topics to me, and his absence from many ongoing events. However, the field notes do contain several comments by staff members and by Rob about Don's concerns with regard to having a girl friend.

It was Pam, Kitty, and Jane who did not show this almost obsessive desire for continuity in having a boyfriend. Jane stayed faithfully with her boyfriend at the workshop and, after he had left, simply stated that there was no one else she was interested in.

During the course of the research, Kitty's interest in boyfriends never developed beyond the "fooling around" stage, and Pam's interest, as has been noted earlier, was focused on dating a staff member. There was no one among the clients who could attract her, so she preferred to have no one.

Table VI shows forty-six observations for the two properties discussed so far (Property A: Desirability, and Property B: Exclusivity). The greater majority of these observations were volunteered. In sum, to have a boy/girl friend gave a great deal of meaning to living. For the majority of the persons, the actualization of it was so important that they continuously attempted to materialize this desire by pursuing a boy/girl friend relation with the "best fit" available, sometimes regardless of other preferences.

One could pose the question: Why would it be so important for less competent persons, living in a group home, to have a boy/girl friend? An obvious answer points to concrete needs that would be fulfilled by the relationship. In the present study, such needs included the need for companionship, talk, and love; the need to have someone to dream about, to be physically intimate with, to receive gifts from; and the need for someone who could give advice. These different meanings given to boy/girl friend relationships have in common a direct concern with daily concrete needs. All subjects but Pam contributed to at least two of these meanings, and Terry, Rob, and Lisa to all. The only negative case came from Pam, who never specified a concrete need involved in her desire to date a staff member. She was very elusive about her dating desires.

Example 80 through 84 illustrate the different meanings the subjects gave to having a boy/girl friend: A boy/girl friend is someone you need, who you miss, who understands you, who loves you, or who is concerned about you.

Example 80: Rob accompanied me to the car. He talked about his stay with his mother over the weekend;

it was sad for him to come back to the cottages as "this is not my home." He went on saying that he might marry his girl friend from the workshop and would soon be looking for an apartment. **Author:** Have you talked with anyone about that? With (name of resident coordinator) or your houseparent? **Rob:** "No, there is no one to talk to. I talk to Teresa." **Author:** Does she understand you? **Rob:** (Looking up at me) "Oh, yes, she understands!" September 3, visit 45)

A boy/girl friend is someone who you are concerned about, who you love, who you try to understand, who misses you, or who needs you.

EXAMPLE 81: When we came back from recreation, Terry invited me up to her room which was now "clean." She was freshly bathed and dressed for the night. She talked for half an hour about her boyfriend: "I can't wait till tomorrow when I can see my boyfriend." Her boyfriend, Max, had had a difficult time and had been taken to the doctor for medication. **Terry:** I feel bad that Max is so weird today. I can't understand him and I really try. It is not nice if one has problems and the other can't understand him. Perhaps it is better for him if he has no girl friend for a while. (May 26, visit 5)
A boy/girl friend is someone you daydream about.

EXAMPLE 82: We were drinking coffee at the roller skating rink. Lisa was clearly not with it for short periods of time. At one point when she seemed to be daydreaming, I asked: What are you daydreaming about? Lisa smiled sweetly and somewhat shyly. **Author:** Or is that private? **Lisa:** No, I am thinking of a certain someone . . . you know, Jimmie. You know him? **Author:** I think so, the person who was at recreation the other day with us? Lisa nodded and smiled. (July 10, visit 28)

A boy/girl friend is someone whose bond with you is expressed in gifts.

EXAMPLE 83: At the workshop I saw Jo-Ann and

another client sitting outside eating lunch. We talked for a moment and I asked about Max. Jo-Ann told me that he was in the hospital but would be back in a week. She added: We are going together. **Author:** "Oh, I thought . . . wasn't he going with Terry?" **Jo-Ann:** Yes, but Terry is now going with Wayne and Max and I are together . . . "see (showing me a ring and necklace), he gave me this." (September 17, visit 51)

A boy/girl friend is someone who gives you guidelines for behavior or acts as an authority figure.

EXAMPLE 84: In the car alone with Lisa, she said she wished that she had a brother. I asked why. **Lisa:** "He would stand up for me. You know . . ." **Author:** Oh, you think a man would do that? **Lisa:** Yes, sure . . . **Author:** Does Jimmie stand up for you? (Jimmie is her boyfriend). **Lisa:** "'Well, he tells me what to do!" **Author:** And do you do it? **Lisa:** "Sometimes, not always" (laughing a little). **Author:** So, who is the boss then? **Lisa:** "It takes two bosses to make a decision, but men do make up your mind though, don't they?" And she added: "And not always the way you like it either." (January 21, visit 89)

The observations discussed so far reflect the fulfillment of concrete, day-to-day needs by having a boy/girl friend. However, there was another major meaning attached to the boy/girl friend concept, which was future oriented. A boy/girl friend was also seen as someone you might marry. To belong to someone as a boy/girl friend seemed to create a sense of continuity, a sense of control over the direction of one's life (however illusionary in the face of the actual fact of no control). For most subjects, even when partners left or shifted, the boy/girl friend concept stayed as a construct with which they strongly identified.

The data suggest that the belief in the possibility of being in a boy/girl friend relationship may well be as important (and perhaps even more so) than the actual fact of having a certain person as a boy/girl friend, because of the projection of continuity into the desired direction of marriage with its promises of independent living and sexual involvement.

The boy/girl friend concept clearly provided a structure from which the subjects derived a sense of stability and control. Its futuristic meaning reinforced and lent credibility to the subjects' projection of marriage; it strengthened their belief in the very possibility of marriage for them, which in turn emphasized the importance of having a boy/girl friend in the first place, completing the circle of perpetual reinforcement of ideas and wishful thinking.

Some subjects used the concept of engagement in expressing this projection of continuity.

> EXAMPLE 85: During a visit to the cottages, Terry expressed her worries about her boyfriend Max who had been taken to the hospital. **Terry:** I was really worried about Max; you know what I mean don't you? Because I love him more than anyone. He is my boyfriend. I have others too . . . Philip, who you met Friday at the workshop . . . and Wayne, but Max comes first. "I love him more than anyone; he is my boyfriend, and we get engaged soon . . . and then we will get married. That is what boyfriend means, doesn't it?" **Author:** Well, I think it means that you know each other for a while first so you can first find out if you really want to get married or . . . not . . . **Terry:** Oh, but I do want to get married to Max and he too. Then he will take care of me. Now he takes care of me as my boyfriend, and I take care of him. He does a good job, and Max says I do a good job taking care of him. (July 9, visit 22)

> EXAMPLE 86: Lisa drew my attention to a ring Jane was wearing. A gold-colored ring from Bill. **Lisa:** She is now engaged. She can't go with any other guy now. And he can't go with any other girl. And they may marry now. **Author:** Is that what engaged means? **Lisa:** "Yes, till they break it up." (June 21, visit 13)

> EXAMPLE 87: In my car on the way to the cottages I saw Max on the street. I offered him a ride. He had been to the hospital by himself for his weekly shots. We

chatted for a while. He then said something about Terry and added: We are engaged. **Author:** Oh, you and Terry . . . when did that happen? **Max:** Last Monday. (September 2, visit 47)

As example 86 shows, the knowledge that the relation may break up was present. In fact, as discussed earlier, some subjects kept a second or third boy/girl friend at hand, so that partners could shift but the "having a boy/girl friend" would continue.

Another meaning given to the boy/girl friend concept related to physical/sexual involvement. A boy/girl friend was clearly seen as someone with whom you could kiss and be more physically intimate. Although these behaviors contributed to fulfillment of concrete needs, they also carried a futuristic function. From the subjects' perspective, a boy/girl friend relationship did not allow for higher levels of physical/sexual intimacies as did marriage (*see* Marriage and physical/sexual involvement). Marriage and its implied sexual behaviors were desired and anticipated. Given that having a boy/girl friend meant increased chances for marriage and thus for unrestricted sexual behavior, the conclusion is that the physical/sexual contacts between boyfriends and girl friends had a function beyond meeting concrete needs: these contacts would lend credibility to the fact that more was to come when the relationship would evolve into marriage. What was still to come was being anticipated and desired.

Examples of observations illustrative of the projective function of the boy/girl friend concept with regard to marriage and its involvement in sexual behavior were offered in the discussion of the Marriage and Physical/Sexual Involvement Pattern (*See,* for instance, examples 36, 37, 38, 39 and 40).

Some additional examples illustrating the physical/sexual meaning given to the boy/girl friend relationship follow.

EXAMPLE 88: Jane is saying that at the workshop they can't do anything. **Jane:** You can't even hold hands. **Lisa:** You can't even go (and gestures a slap on one's bottom) or anything. **Author:** What if you lived alone, say in an apartment, could you kiss your boyfriend? **Lisa:** Oh, yes, then you can kiss and hug." (November 15, visit 68)

EXAMPLE 89: On my first visit to the women's cottage, the houseparent asked Jane and Lisa to show me their rooms. We went upstairs to the room they shared. On the wall was a picture of a man and woman kissing each other. **Jane:** You know what that makes me think of? **Author:** No. **Jane:** "My boyfriend and me" (giggling a little). **Lisa:** "Or my boyfriend and me." **Jane:** Her boyfriend is Jimmie. **Author:** Do you see your boyfriends often? **Lisa:** "He works at the workshop. Sometimes he kisses me." (May 23, visit 2)

EXAMPLE 90: Rob is talking about his possible marriage with his girl friend. **Author:** Does she want to marry you too? **Rob:** "Yes, she does – I kissed her Friday you know" (looking up at me, flushing a little). (September 3, visit 45)

In addition, there were many observations noted in the field notes of actual involvement by boy/girl friends in kissing, hugging, holding hands, and sitting closely. Example 91 is illustrative of such observations:

EXAMPLE 91: Max had just returned from the hospital but was tired and did not want to go to social club. Terry sat and talked very seriously with him for quite a while. When we were about to leave she got up, kissed him, and joined us. (June 9, visit 9)

Several other observations are noted of such behaviors between Jane and Bill, Max and Terry, and Lisa and Jimmie.

Table VI shows that five properties were generated under the category Boy/Girl Friend emerging from 127 observations. Thus, an average of three incidents were observed every two visits. Also, the greater majority of the verbal statements (72%) were volunteered. In sum, this pattern indicates that having a boy/girl friend carried utmost meaning for most, if not all persons, of this study.

Discussion

The pattern discussed above adds evidence to Henshel's (1972, p. 180) impression that personalities in dating and marriage matter relatively little: "We often had the impression that the personalities involved mattered little. Because a boy met a girl under certain circumstances, marriage was at the end of the journey and each had to follow the direction of the road no matter who the co-traveler was." Likewise, Edgerton (1967) notes that his subjects would marry anyone. While these statements seem extreme, the data of the present research indicate that the same may equally apply to the subjects of this study with regard to the boy/girl friend they choose. Just to have one was of great importance: a boy/girl friend starts you on the road to marriage, which, as other patterns discussed in this chapter showed, is an important status to gain for its own sake. Viewing oneself as part of a boy/girl friend relationship was for most subjects so important that they would engage in such relationships with "the best fit" available and would attempt to replace the partner when necessary.

It may be of interest to compare Henshel's (1977) findings with the data of this pattern. Henshel found that the most important meaning of dating was to have someone in order to enjoy the most exciting pastimes, such as eating out, going to movies, parties, and dances, since in this culture, these types of entertainment are centered around the couple. The subjects in the present study did not assign this meaning to having a boy/girl friend. In their setting they enjoyed these very activities as a group. They did not necessarily need a boy/girl friend to engage in them. Instead, they mentioned other ways in which having a boy/girl friend was meaningful to them in their daily lives. It may be, of course, that both studies were able to detect only the one set of meanings. However, it is more likely that they articulated the most prominent meanings in the particular behavioral setting. This again emphasizes the need for naturalistic studies when investigating meaning in the lives of persons labeled retarded.

Chapter 5

INTERPERSONAL UNDERSTANDING

SEVERAL PROPERTIES showed relations that reflected a desire to understand someone else's behavior, actual understanding of another person's behavior, and ways in which such understanding was used. Figure 10 shows the pattern of these relations.

While properties A, B, and C have in common an actual understanding of another person's behavior, the motivations for doing so differ as well as the manifestations of such understanding. Property A (Giving advice or help, showing insight or concern, based upon knowledge of the other person's needs) emerged from observations in which there were no observable benefits for the actor. Example 92 through 95 are representative of the twenty-five observations from which this property emerged:

> EXAMPLE 92: Max and I were talking in the refreshment area of the roller skating rink. Suddenly Terry (his girl friend) came to our table, grabbed her purse which was laying on the table, and walked off very angrily. Max looked up: "Terry!," and added: What was that? He hurried to take his roller skates off and said to me: Would you go and see what is wrong, she must be upset. (July 10, visit 28)

> EXAMPLE 93. We were sitting in the living room in the women's cottage (Lisa, Terry, and myself). Terry goes into a big tirade about how Kitty gets in her way and bosses her around. She does not want Kitty to be her roommate anymore. Lisa says Kitty is saying the same about Terry and advises Terry to "lay all the cards open on the table so Kitty knows that Terry does not like her

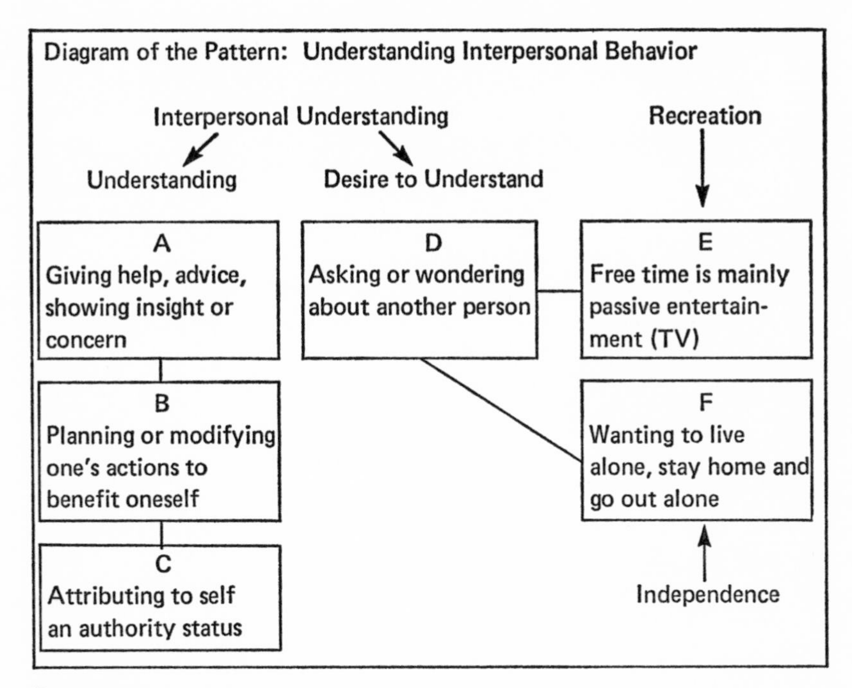

DEFINITIONS

Category: Interpersonal Understanding: Any act or verbal statement reflecting a meaning the subjects gave to the understanding of another person's behavior.

Property A: Giving advice or help, showing insight or concern, based upon knowledge of the other person's need.

B: Planning or modifying one's actions based upon an understanding of another person's situation to benefit oneself.

C: Attributing to oneself an authority status based upon the understanding of the other person's behavioral limitations.

D: Asking another person about his/her life or behavior, or wondering about another person's behavior.

Category: Recreation: Any act or verbal statement reflecting a meaning the subjects gave to recreation (including organized recreation, leisure time, travel time).

Property E: Free time primarily means passive entertainment (TV).

Category: Independence: Any act or verbal statement reflecting a meaning the subjects gave to being free or wanting to be free from control of others as they knew such control in their existing situation.

Property F: Wanting to live alone, or "to-be-on-my-own." Wanting to stay home unsupervised and wanting to come home and go out without having to account for it.

Figure 10.

Table VII

Frequency Distribution of Observations of the Pattern: Understanding Interpersonal Behavior

*Properties**	*Men*	*Women*	*Total*
	(n=3)	(n=5)	
A. Giving help, advice, showing insight, or concern	10	18	28
B. Planning or modifying one's actions to benefit oneself	11	13	24
C. Attributing to self an authority status	11	6	17
D. Asking or wondering about another person	8	17	25
	40	54	94
E. Free time is mainly passive entertainment (TV)	16	29	45
F. Wanting to live alone, stay home and go out alone	15	31	46
Total	71	114	185

*The volunteered-elicited condition is not applicable for the observations coded under the Properties A, B, C, and D. The events in these observations are voluntary in nature. Most meaning-indicators under Property E consisted of acts (the act of watching TV) and the volunteered-elicited condition for Property F has no impact on this pattern.

and Terry knows that Kitty does not like her . . . and that's it . . . just leave it with that." When Terry goes on complaining, Lisa continues: Well, go to ——— (resident coordinator), not when he is in a hurry, but after all his work is done so he has time for you, and sit down and tell him all your troubles with Kitty and he can help. (July 3, visit 18)

EXAMPLE 94: Bob (nonsubject) is trying to put a clean plastic bag in the kitchen garbage can. He is fumbling with it. **Don:** "No, Bob, do it this way." He turns the bag the right way and helps to put it in. Bob leaves with the garbage. **Author:** He does not know how to do it? **Don:** "Sometimes he gets confused; he does it inside out." (November 3, visit 62)

EXAMPLE 95: The librarian was showing Rob how to run the film projector. She did something wrong. **Librarian:** "Shit . . . oh sorry . . . shoot!" **Rob:** "Don't worry. I use these words myself." (July 26, visit 29)

Observations that gave rise to Property B (Planning or modifying one's actions based upon an understanding of another person's situation to benefit oneself) are characterized by a manipulative orientation. Sometimes, the manipulative element was rather subtle, and I came to observe more incidents as I became better acquainted with the situation and with the subjects. For instance, Don's style was to carefully build up an indirect request, and it took careful attention on the part of the listener to detect the purpose of his conversation. He would not say explicitly what he wanted. It seemed as if he wanted to keep the freedom to pull back at any moment without losing face. Once I saw how he did this, I observed him doing it on several occasions with staff members and other subjects. Example 96 illustrates Don's tactic.

EXAMPLE 96: I am alone with Don in the kitchen. **Don:** What are you planning for next week? **Author:** I don't know, just getting ready for Christmas, and some work to do. **Don:** "But next Tuesday and Wednesday?" **Author:** What is so special about Tuesday and Wednesday? **Don:** "Well, it is home coming. There are two games." I asked him whether he was going. **Don:** "No . . ." Then he added: Last year someone took me. I asked him where it was. He told me and said again that he went last year. I still had not caught on. It was quiet for a few seconds and then Don said again: "Last year someone took me." **Author:** Well, I could take you there and go with you. Don looked up but did not answer and went right on working, preparing food. **Author:** Would you like that? **Don:** Yes! (December 15, visit 71)

Rob would apply a similar tactic, though a little more direct. Rob was seen by the staff as particularly clever in manipulation. For instance, the weekend houseparent related the following story: Rob had woken him up early Sunday morning, and said

"I'm going to church, my ——— (name of relative) is here to get me. I'll be back after church." The houseparent had said "OK" not realizing until later that Rob was not to go until noon according to the rule. He did not reappear until after church in the evening, justifying himself by the fact that he had said: "I'll be back after church." Since Rob goes to church twice on Sundays, he had covered himself by saying "after church" while knowing that he would not have been permitted to stay out all day if he had specified an exact time. The houseparent found himself in a bind, as he had agreed to Rob coming home after church. Example 97 is taken from the field notes:

> EXAMPLE 97: I left the men's cottage (where Rob and some others were present) after I had mentioned that I was going home. I dropped in at the women's cottage, where Kitty was watching television. Rob came in and said: Oh, I want to make it over to cross-town, but it might start raining. That is a hot walk. (It dawned upon me that he was indirectly asking for a ride. I did not offer one to see what he was going to do.) After a few minutes, he said: Are you going to stay around here? **Author:** Just a little, I'd like to see a bit of this program. **Rob:** So, when are you going ? What direction are you going? **Author:** Oooh, you want a ride? **Rob:** Yes. (July 6, visit 20)

Other subjects were more direct and transparent about their attempts to use knowledge of others to benefit themselves.

> EXAMPLE 98: When I entered the women's cottage, Lisa mentioned something to which Kitty responded: "Watch out! There she is." **Lisa:** "I don't care if she knows, but I don't want John (houseparent) to know." (August 16, visit 36)

> EXAMPLE 99: I am taking Don to the nearby supermarket to practice grocery shopping. The others are getting ready to go to a fair. Jane lingers around and says, looking at me and at the houseparent: "I would like to see how people do the grocery shopping." (October 18, visit 57)

EXAMPLE 100: Upon leaving the cottages late at night, I talked a few minutes with the houseparent in the parking lot. Someone came running past the parking lot to the cottages. It was Max. **Houseparent:** "Hey, Max, why are you running . . . for me?" **Max:** No, I am just in time. I did not want you to worry about where I am." (September 20, visit 52)

EXAMPLE 101: We were sitting in the refreshment areas of the roller skating rink – Lisa, Pam, Jane, and myself. We got coffee, except Pam. She did not have any money. I offered to lend her some. She accepted and said she would pay me back, adding: If she (recreation worker) knows, she gets mad again. (Pam never paid me back; the recreation worker had related to me previously that Pam tries to borrow money without returning it.) (July 10, visit 28)

An interesting group of observations is subsumed under Property C: "Attributing to oneself an authority status based upon the understanding of the other person's behavioral limitations." The benefit here is psychological in nature. In the previous discussed property the subjects received something tangible from their manipulation (being taken to a ball game, getting a ride, the chance to go grocery shopping, no punishment for being late, and free coffee). Here they obtain the psychological satisfaction of being in authority. The authority relation consistently took place between the subjects and nonsubjects who were at a distinctly lower level of functioning, at least verbally. Bossing around also occurred among the subjects; however, there it was not effective in that it was met with resistance and counteractions. Such observations were not included, as the behaviors did not represent real authority but merely resembled quarreling. In the observations from which Property C emerged, there was always a final acceptance of authority.

EXAMPLE 102: John comes in and has his hands on his crotch, as usual. **Rob:** John! Keep your hands on your back . . . and keep them there!" John obeys. (December 1, visit 70)

EXAMPLE 103: We had arrived at the restaurant with

all subjects to eat dinner. Everyone sat down except Bob who was wandering around. **Kitty:** "Here Bob, sit down!" **Jane:** "No Bob, sit here next to me." Bob sat down next to Jane. (August 10, visit 36)

EXAMPLE 104: During structured recreation Tim started "flying" (a typical behavior for him where he ran around moving his arms like a bird's wings). Terry immediately told him to calm down. A little later after the exercises that we engaged in were over, Terry, sitting next to me on the benches, said: ""Tim, come here!" Tim immediately came over. **Terry:** "I want to talk to you. What is bothering you tonight? What is your problem?" Tim stuttered something about work (I could not understand it). **Terry:** "Well, that is over now. Go, and I'll buy a coke if you are good . . ." **Tim:** "Yesss . . ." (September 20, visit 52)

EXAMPLE 105: Tim had entered the living room where Rob is playing his records. He goes to the records and touches them, halfway picking them up. Rob flares up, but without words. He points his finger at the chair and Tim immediately obeys and sits down. No words were said. Rob looks straight at Tim a moment and then continues with his records as if nothing had happened. (July 31, visit 31)

EXAMPLE 106: Don is in the kitchen preparing food. John came in, his pants hanging halfway down, as is typical. **Don:** "John, pull up your pants!" while he pulled up John's pants from the back. John pulled up his pants. The houseparent entered the kitchen area and said: Come on Don, John has enough bosses here. **Don:** Yes, but his pants are falling down if he does not pull them up. Wouldn't that be funny (laughing)? (December 15, visit 71)

All subjects but Pam contributed to this pattern. It was probably because Pam was a loner that I did not obtain any observations from her. She rarely participated in a group setting.

The pattern shows a distinct difference between the sexes with regard to their contribution to Property C (Attributing to oneself an authority status) : there were eleven for the men and six for the women. Especially since there were three men and five women, this difference is interesting and may be a function of greater male aggressiveness according to traditional stereotypes.

The data discussed so far (69 observations for the Properties A, B, and C) showed ways in which the subjects used their particular understanding of another person's behavior. The field notes also contained data that showed the subjects in the process of acquiring knowledge about another person. Table VII shows twenty-five observations from which the Property "Asking another person about his/her life or behavior, or wondering about another person's behavior" emerged. When examining these observations it immediately became apparent that the majority of them were questions directed at me. In nineteen of the observations, subjects asked about certain aspects of my life. (During the course of the research there were more questions which I did not take down, as they became repetitive and my attention was focused elsewhere.) It was certainly not surprising that they asked these questions, as I was a new person in their lives about whom they knew nothing. However, the content of their questions seemed particularly interesting. Seventeen of the nineteen questions posed dealt with the following: (1) Where are your children? Are they alone? (2) Do you trust them home alone? (3) Are they watching television? and (4) What would they be doing? (after I responded that we didn't have a television). The subjects had met my nine- and ten-year-old children on several occasions. The children had been invited by a houseparent to come on a picnic, and they were present when the subjects visited my home. In addition, they played around the cottages several times with a son of the houseparent who was their classmate.

> Example 107: Don is sitting about five feet away from me on the benches during structured recreation watching the others play ball; I am keeping score. He is looking at me for quite a while and asks: "'Where are your children?" (September 20, visit 52)

EXAMPLE 108: During a visit to the house of a recreation worker, we are sitting around with juice and cookies. **Kitty:** "Where are your kids?" I tell her that they are home. **Kitty:** Are they home alone? **Author:** Yes. **Kitty:** What are they doing, watching television? **Author:** No, I don't have a television. They are probably reading or playing a game or riding their bikes. **Rob:** (Who has overheard this) "Do you trust them?" **Author:** "Yes, I am just starting to leave them home alone from time to time when I am not going to be home too late. (September 6, visit 46)

EXAMPLE 109: I enter the women's cottage where Kitty, Lisa, and Terry are watching television. **Kitty:** "Hi Lous, where are your children, are they playing?" **Lisa:** "Are they alone? Do you trust them?" (November 6, visit 68)

Though all subjects but Pam asked these questions, it was particularly Kitty, Lisa, and Rob who were very interested. Kitty especially would almost automatically ask about my children. The most obvious explanation seems to be the fact that Kitty had a child of her own and perhaps projected her thoughts about her own child. One could also speculate that the commonality between us of having a child, which none of the other subjects shared, might have provided reinforcement in her belief that she belonged to the "normal" side of life.

Properties generated under different categories show an interesting relation to the subjects' rather narrowly focused interest in my children. These are the properties under the category Recreation "Free time means primarily passive entertainment (TV)", and the combined properties under the category Independence "Wanting to live alone or to be on my own" and "Wanting to stay home unsupervised and wanting to come and go out without having to account for it." While my children used their free time in many ways, the subjects could not imagine what to do without a television and went to bed at 8:30 when the television was broken. While my children were trusted to stay home alone, several of the adult subjects were not. The chapter on Independence (Chapter

3) provided examples of the subjects' desire for greater independent living. The following examples illustrate the importance of television as a means to spend free time.

> EXAMPLE 110: We are sitting in the living room, talking and watching television (Terry, Lisa, Kitty, and the houseparent). Terry starts talking about her family. **Houseparent:** "Remember, we would not talk about our families." **Kitty:** "We talk about something happy, like the movie on television." (November 15, visit 68)

> EXAMPLE 111: From attendance at a staff meeting: The television broke. It seems to be rather disastrous. They (subjects) now go to bed at 8:30 (December 1, visit 70)

> EXAMPLE 112: Don asked me what my favorite television program was. I told him I rarely watched and that I didn't have a television. **Don:** "Someone should give you one." I said that I did not particularly care for a television. **Don:** "Well, it would come in handy sometime." I agreed to that possibility. (August 20, visit 37)

> EXAMPLE 113: After Lisa and I came back from our trip downtown we talked for a few minutes in the cottage. She asked how my children were and whether they were alone now and what they were doing. She said: "I wonder how they occupy their time. (She knows I don't have a television.) I bet they would like to have a television of their own." (January 21, visit 81)

For all practical purposes, the television set was on constantly. Also, the furniture in the rooms was arranged around the television set.

Although there is no direct bearing on the pattern being discussed, it may be of interest to note the kind of programs the subjects typically saw. Occasionally the educational channel was watched for a special program, but ordinarily, the subjects saw the kind of programs listed below. For three consecutive weeks in November, four days a week (Monday through Thursday), the following programs were viewed: "Brady Bunch" (11×), "Andy

Griffith Show" (10×), "Hogan's Heroes" (11×), "The Odd Couple" (11×), "Mulligan Stew" (1×), "Emergency One" (6×), "Eight is Enough" (3×), "Charlie's Angels" (3×), "Flintstones" (3×), "Three Stooges" (4×), "Little House on the Prairie" (2×), basketball game (1×), evening movies (4×).

The purpose of this study was not to investigate how ways of giving meaning to living came into being, but rather to study what they were. It was not feasible to include the former question, though such investigation would seem most relevant. Given the extensive exposure to television (70 programs in 12 days), it may well have been that television (and some occasional movies in town), and the kind of programs they watched, helped to shape the ways the subjects came to invest their day-to-day life with meaning. Some observations from the field notes would suggest this possibility.

> Example 114: I am talking with Jane and Lisa in the living room. I ask Jane what kind of work her mother does. Jane tells us that her mother is a secretary. **Lisa:** "Does she sit on her boss's lap? Does her boss chase her around the office?" **Author:** Where do you get that idea? **Lisa:** "Oh, I watch the movies." She then repeats the question to Jane. Jane shrugs her shoulders and shakes her head. **Author:** Do you think that really happens? **Lisa:** "Oh, yes, sometimes. I see it on the movies you know." (January 5, visit 77)

Clearly, extensive television watching is also typical of our society at large. The question may be whether television could have a differential impact when behavioral settings differ. For instance, persons we label retarded and place in a strictly supervised setting have very little, if any, exposure to the real-life world of independent living, marriage, rearing children, and sexual involvement with which one normally can counterbalance (to some extent at least) the impressions flowing from the television set. At the same time these persons desire very much to experience these aspects of life. Thus, with little or no exposure on the one hand, and a great desire to experience on the other, television may shape the ways these persons regard independent living, marriage, and related issues, in a manner which we do not know but which may be important to investigate if we want to understand how persons like the subjects of this study come to view life as meaningful.

Discussion

The patterns of Interpersonal Understanding resemble the findings by Braginski and Braginski (1971) and Edgerton and Sabagh (1962). Braginski and Braginski (1971) showed that persons in institutions for the retarded are effective in interpersonal manipulation in experimental situations. For example, these researchers created a situation in which the subjects could misrepresent their IQ scores in order to "cop out" of or to enter a hypothetical educational program. Subjects were given an IQ test and were asked to retake the test. Before taking the test the second time, the experimental subjects were informed that persons with a high IQ would be enrolled in an educational program which was described as very structured and very demanding. Persons with a low IQ would not be enrolled. Although the group means did not change, thirty-four of the experimental subjects showed a change of two years in mental age between test 1 and test 2, while no similar change in mental age occurred for control subjects. Braginski and Braginski conclude that the treatment did influence the subjects to play the "now bright—then dumb" game. While the kind of post-hoc analysis employed by Braginski and Braginski may be open to question, the interpretations of the results are intriguing and reflect the ability for understanding social situations and interpersonal manipulation. The findings of the present study can be seen as complementing Braginski and Braginski's findings in terms of the different research paradigm by which they were obtained.

A study by Edgerton and Sabagh (1962) discusses the "self-aggrandizement" function of interpersonal manipulation by persons in an institution. These authors observed the same kind of behaviors from which in the present study the property "Attributing to oneself an authority status based upon the understanding of the other person's behavioral limitation" emerged. The rather ample opportunity to compare oneself with someone who is even "dumber" is a situation most persons have probably not experienced before entering the institution or group home. Edgerton and Sabagh (1962, p. 268) state:

> The realization that many others are less intelligent must be highly satisfying, for patients quickly and enthusiastically learn to refer to the more retarded persons as "low-grades," a term of utmost opprobrium; indeed, they are taught this term by employees. When the low-grades are not being vilified and abused, they are patronizingly being given aid in simple tasks. On every hand, the relatively greater retardation of their fellow patients serves to raise the mildly retarded patients' concepts of their own intellectual ability. As a rather predictable consequence, they conclude that the stigma "mental defect" properly applies to the severely retarded only, and they are enabled to deny that they belong in the hospital at all.

Thus, the pattern discussed in this chapter concurs with Braginski and Braginski (1971) and Edgerton and Sabagh (1962) in showing ability for interpersonal manipulation. In addition, it points to the less self-centered ways in which knowledge of other persons is used—by expressing concern, insight, and offering help and advice.

The important point made in these studies, for theoretical as well as practical purposes, is that the persons we place in institutional or group home settings do learn to understand complex situations, acquire knowledge of other persons, and can adapt their behavior accordingly.

Chapter 6

INTRAPERSONAL UNDERSTANDING

THIS CHAPTER addresses the question of how the subjects gave meaning to their status as a retardate. Their message was clear: I'm here, and I don't know how to do everything, but I am not retarded. However, the topic was a touchy one for discussion, to say the least. Only once was the word "retarded" voluntarily mentioned by Lisa with reference to someone else and still within the context of a conversation about her own status as a mental retardate. Nor was their status as a retardate discussed with them by the staff members. There were strict rules at the workshop against calling names, and referral to each other as "retarded" was thought of by the subjects as sufficient reason to be fired.

Conversations with the subjects about the appropriateness of the label "retarded" were not initiated until the latter part of the research period. There had been a total absence of remarks about their status as mental retardates, whether among themselves, with staff members, or with me. However, it was clear that these persons were well aware of being judged not competent to manage their own lives. The data collected had shown their awareness of their strictly supervised lives and their dependence. In most concrete terms, their environment showed them daily that they had been judged retarded: the following words were clearly printed on the bus which took their fellow clients of the workshop to and from work: "(Name) Council for Retarded Citizens." The reading skills of several subjects, though most elementary, were sufficient to read the label.

Thus, during the latter part of the study I found opportunities to initiate conversations with all the subjects but Don, and to talk about their perceptions of their competence. These conversations rendered some interesting results from which the property: "Denying one's status as a mental retardate" emerged. Together with other properties, it gave rise to the pattern in Figure 11.

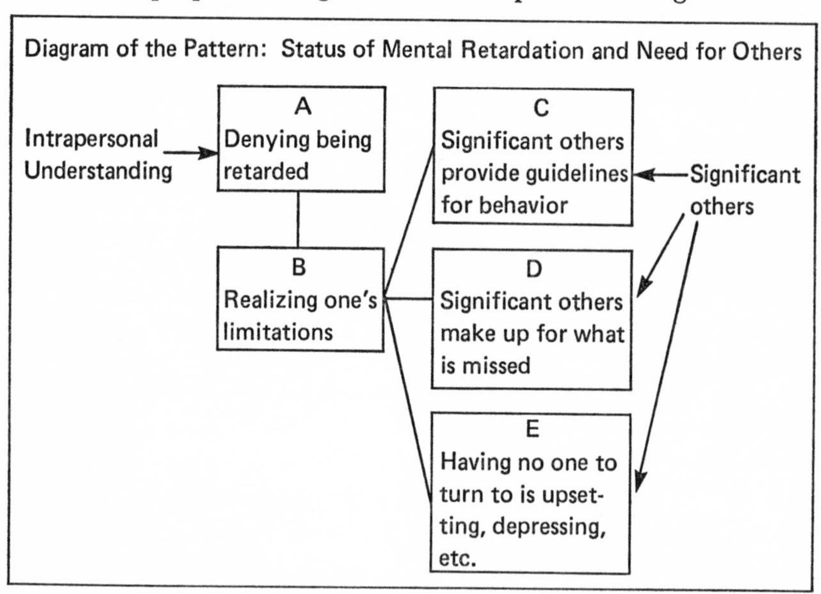

DEFINITIONS

Category: Intrapersonal Understanding: Any act or verbal statement reflecting a meaning the subjects gave to their own behavior: thoughts, feelings, and reflections about its limitations, boundaries, motivations, or possible consequences.

Property A: Denying one's status as a mental retardate.

B: Realization of one's own limitations (in living skills, academic skills, in knowledge, or emotional maturity).

Category: Significant Others: Any act or verbal statement reflecting a meaning the subjects gave to a mother, father, other relative, a family or other important persons.

Property C: Significant others provide guidelines for behavior or act as authority figures.

D: Living with significant others, or having contact with them (such as weekend visits) is seen as making up for what seems to be lacking in the present situation.

E: Significant others are persons who are there when you need them; not having any such person to turn to is upsetting and depressing.

Figure 11.

STATUS OF MENTAL RETARDATION AND NEED FOR OTHERS

Table VIII shows ten observations indicating denial of one's status as a mental retardate. In this particular case, some rather lengthy conversations were considered as single observations, since these observations were very focused and a result of extensive probing.

Table VIII

Frequency Distribution of Observations of the Pattern:
Status of Mental Retardation and Need for Others

Properties	*Volunteered*	*Elicited*	*Total*
A. Denying being retarded	1	9	10
B. Realizing one's limitations	20	9	29
C. Significant others provide guidelines for behavior	25	3	28
D. Significant others make up for what is missed	15	4	19
E. Having no one to turn to is upsetting, depressing, etc.	7	1	8
Total	68	26	94

The following segments of the field notes illustrate the subjects perceptions of their competence.

EXAMPLE 115: While walking with Pam to the concert hall we are talking about the workshop. **Author:** Now, ---- (name of workshop) is called the school for retarded citizens. Do you consider yourself retarded? **Pam:** "No, I don't. I am not retarded." **Author:** Do you think that some persons at the workshop are retarded? **Pam:** "Oh, some are." (October 26, visit 59)

EXAMPLE 116: Up in Terry's room, I am talking with Jane, Lisa, and Kitty. Terry is lying on her bed, half asleep. The others are talking about the workshop. I ask the question about considering themselves retarded, since they are in a group home and work in the workshop for "retarded citizens." **Lisa:** "No, I am not retarded . . . I am tired — but not retarded!" (halfway making fun of it). **Jane:** (Shaking her head) "No, I am not retarded either." Kitty merely shook her head and said: "No". I then asked them what that word meant to them. **Lisa:** Retarded means that . . . "you learn slow. But I learn and Jane also." I asked what they were learning. **Lisa:** "Sorting zippers and paper." **Author:** Are those important things to learn you think? **Lisa:** "Oh, yes . . . they *are important.*" I asked whether people ever call each other retarded at work or in the cottages. **Lisa:** They call each each other turkey, but not when the supervisors hear it. **Author:** Why not? **Lisa:** You would be fired. She then told me with interjections from Jane and Kitty that someone had been fired because of calling other people names. (January 5, visit 77)

Lisa's attaching importance to learning how to sort zippers and Jane's attaching importance to sorting paper were clear rationalizations. They both knew. They had been on the same job for four and seven years respectively. Kitty had been breaking glass every day for five years. Both Lisa and Jane had expressed their dislike for their work on several other occasions:

EXAMPLE 117: During lunch at the workshop, I saw Lisa coming down the hall. She had tears in her eyes. I asked what was the matter. **Lisa:** I am not feeling well, everything is yellow. I hate it here. It is not good here. (August 8, visit 34)

EXAMPLE 118: Terry was in the kitchen complaining to the houseparent about work. The houseparent touched her lips and said teasingly: perhaps you should not use this so much and work more. **Terry:** No, I don't like it. **Jane:** "You know what I don't like? Tearing paper and taking stickers off and . . . and . . ." (two more things I could not understand). That is what I hate." And she adds: "I like to be a waitress." **Author:** A waitress? (to be sure I understood her correctly). **Jane:** "Yes, and wait on people . . . or a babysitter . . ."* (September 13, visit 49)

If Lisa and Jane were to deny their status as mental retardates and being mentally retarded meant learning slowly then they had to prove that they were learning and were learning something that was important. To acknowledge that they were not learning anything could be acknowledging membership in the category retarded.

The next conversation is with Terry at a coffee shop after attending a concert:

> EXAMPLE 119: Terry talked about the workshop. **Author:** Now the workshop is called a workshop for the retarded. What does that word mean to you? Terry looked a little taken back (I think) and said: "Well, that you learn slow, and that you can't read or write." **Author:** Do you think of yourself as retarded? **Terry:** "No, I can read and write . . . a little." **Author:** Are there others who you think are retarded? **Terry:** Wayne, maybe. **Author:** Why is that? **Terry:** "He talks weird sometimes." I asked if anyone ever used the word retarded at the workshop or in the cottages. Terry said no one ever did and added: "You probably would get fired!" (November 16, visit 69)

Because she could read and write a little, Terry likewise denied the appropriateness of the above definition of the label retarded for herself. However, Terry's reading and writing skills amounted to little, if anything. She could read and write only the most elementary words.

A conversation with Rob is presented in the next example:

> EXAMPLE: 120: I am driving back with Rob from the roller skating rink. We started talking about the workshop. I asked my usual introductory question: You are there. Do you consider yourself retarded? **Rob:** "Me?

*It should be noted that not all subjects disliked working in the workshop as much as Jane, Terry, and Lisa. For these three subjects, the workshop also offered pleasant aspects, such as contact with friends.

No! I am not retarded and I hate that word. My mother does not want anyone to call me that and I don't want it." He added: Sometimes they call me "sighthead." **Author:** What? **Rob:** "Sighthead." I asked what that meant. **Rob:** Oh . . . (mumbled something). **Author:** Does it mean something like retarded? **Rob:** Yes. I asked where they had called him so. **Rob:** At the workshop. I asked whether they could call each other names there. **Rob:** Oh, no. **Author:** What does the word retarded mean to you? **Rob:** (After a second) "Nothing! It doesn't mean nothing to me!" **Author:** Does it matter then that you have been labeled retarded? **Rob:** "Yes I hate it." **Author:** Aren't you telling me then that it must mean something to you? Can you say what it means to you? Rob did not answer. **Author:** Let me ask it this way: Are there persons at the workshop who you think are retarded? **Rob:** Yes, some perhaps. **Author:** What makes them retarded in your eyes? **Rob:** "Well, they can't do much of anything." **Author:** I see . . . you see, so many people use the word retarded differently, and I am interested in how you see it. It was silent for a minute and I picked up on the conversation. "Now, you are at the workshop. Why do *you* think you are there? **Rob:** "Well, I went . . ." from there on he mumbled and I could not quite follow what he said. It had to do with not learning too well at school. At that point we passed by a supermarket and he switched the topic of conversation by asking me if he could go in to buy cigarettes. He did.

Back in the car I picked up the converasation once more. I mentioned that I had heard someone using the word "normal adult" and asked him whether he considered himself a normal adult. **Rob:** "I'm trying to be." **Author:** Does that mean that you are not quite a normal adult in your eyes? **Rob:** "Yes, I am; I am a normal adult." **Author:** What are you trying to do in order to be a normal adult? **Rob:** "Oh, clean the place, wash, cook . . ." **Author:** Does that make you a normal adult?

Rob: Yes, then I can live alone. **Author:** What other things does a normal adult do who lives alone? **Rob:** "Sleeps, works, goes out . . ." **Author:** Does he marry? **Rob:** If he wants to, yes. I asked him whether he thought the other persons in the cottages were normal adults. **Rob:** "No." **Author:** Are they retarded in your eyes? **Rob:** "No, they are not retarded either." **Author:** When they get a place of their own, would you say they would be normal adults? **Rob:** "Yes, they would." The conversation ended there; we had arrived at the cottages. (January 3, visit 76)

The conversation with Rob is a clear illustration of the subjects' dilemma: I am not retarded, but I must not be quite normal either. To "try to be normal" meant to Rob to do what staff members told him he had to learn: cook, wash, and clean. Mastering these skills would allow him to live alone one day—or so the message had come across—and thus be normal, that is, not retarded anymore. Clearly, while Rob says that the word retarded means "Nothing!" it means a great deal. Lisa, in the next conversation, expresses similar perceptions:

Examples 121: I had taken Lisa to the bank and then to the coffee shop. We were twenty minutes before serving time, so we just talked. She talked about her sister with whom she stayed for Christmas, who had three daughters. **Lisa:** "And the fifteen year old calls us names; she says: 'The creeps at ——— (name of the workshop)' . . . and that is bad! That is showing no respect! And I told her: 'That's enough young lady!' " Lisa added: She asked me if my boyfriend was also retarded . . . now, that is no respect at all!

A little later in the conversation she repeated the story about her niece. I asked her what the word retarded really meant to her. **Lisa:** "When you learn slow, I think." **Author:** Now take John, he does not speak . . . **Lisa:** (Interrupting) "He is very bright. He understands everything . . ." **Author:** Would you consider him retarded? **Lisa:** "In a way, yes, but then, no, he is really bright," and added: he knows everything you say, but he can't see well. He is a mongoloid; you know what that is, don't you? Before I had the chance to answer she explained that one's eyes are bad when one is a mongoloid. I told her that I heard someone use the word "normal adult." She immediately jumped and said: "Normal! Who is to say what is normal?" **Author:** Would you consider John a normal adult then? **Lisa:** "Well, yes, he just has a handicap." **Author:** And yourself? **Lisa:** "I am, yes." I told her that I would like to ask again why she thought she was at the workshop; what were her troubles? **Lisa:** Well, I learn maybe a little slow. In a way I have a handicap you may say, but I am doing really well in VR (vocational rehabilitation), and she added: My supervisor showed me my production sheet. "I am trying my best. That is all you can do." I asked her what she would have to do to be an adult without handicaps. **Lisa:** I would go to college. I could take summer courses. My sister says I could be a supervisor, or a spelling teacher; I am very good in spelling (she is indeed). I just don't have a degree. See, I had to quit junior high. The doctors told me to stop school for a while as I was nervous. I am not good in math. I am also lazy. I could be a teacher if I was not so lazy. (January 21, visit 81)

By saying ". . . who is to say what is normal!" Lisa would have agreed with Blatt's (1977, p. 7) statement: "In the beginning humans were created and then humans created the criteria for being human."

Clearly, the fact that the subjects' status as a mental retardate was never openly discussed or initiated was not a function of its unimportance or of the subjects' ignorance. Rather, the topic, in terms of straightforward discussion, seemed to be shunned. Discussing it seriously meant to have to come up with rationalizations for being where they were or to accept the label retarded, which seemed the last thing they wanted to do. To accept the label would mean to acknowledge that they were in the right place.

As the examples illustrate, I tried to weave two questions into the conversations: why were the subjects there, and what did being normal mean. The first question elicited various answers, all providing reasons for being there other than retardation. Pam said that she and her mother did not get along and were always fighting, Terry said that she was there because her father and mother broke up and she had no place to go; Max could "not figure it out;" Kitty simply did not know; Jane might "pass out" if she would be home alone, and since her mother worked, she would have to be alone sometimes; Lisa thought she was in the cottage because if she were home, she would be lonely, and her sister and brother-in-law (her guardians) felt she would be happier with "her peers;" Rob never provided a clear answer except for mumbling something about not learning well in school; Don refused to respond and, shrugging his shoulders, said "I don't know" in his typically evasive manner.

Edgerton (1967) and Braginski and Braginski (1971) list some similar rationalizations used by their subjects to account for their institutionalization, which included alcoholism, epilepsy or other physical illnesses, nervousness, sex delinquency, and abandonment by relatives.

Only Rob and Lisa came up with answers to the question: what does it mean to be normal? Their responses were: living alone, going to college, being a teacher, and marrying—these were seen as things normal people do. I asked this question one way or another to all subjects but Don, and except for Lisa and Rob, an answer was avoided. They either could not or would not verbalize their thoughts. This was one point in the research where further probing seemed unethical. I felt that further questioning might have reinforced the idea that they were not normal. Why else would I ask? Thus, further questioning was dropped when faced with an "I don't know" answer. Continuation might have put them in a bind. It may be that to specify normalcy for someone who has been judged retarded, who knows that s/he is in a place for the retarded and who denies that status, would force him/her to accept that status. In other words, to specify normalcy would not be possible in terms of their actual living conditions. To specify normalcy in ways other than their actual living conditions would be to acknowledge that they did not meet the requirements. This double bind may have made it impossible for these persons to clearly state what being normal meant to them.

The data in this study may present the subjects' view of normalcy, since it seems patent that their conception of normalcy can be seen from the ways they wanted to live differently than their retarded status (which they denied) allowed them to. Since they did not want to be labeled retarded, they wished for living conditions that, from their perspective, would put them in a situation in which they would not be seen as retarded. The logic in this reasoning is as follows:

- The subjects deny being retarded;
- They know that they live and work in places where they are judged retarded;
- They cannot specify what it means to be normal since such specification is not possible in terms of their actual living conditions and to specify normalcy in terms of anything else would be to acknowledge that they are not that;
- Therefore, they wish for living conditions that would make them "not-retarded."

An answer to the question, What do they want differently? can be quickly found from examining their behavioral patterns discussed in this research. It was seen that much of the subjects' energy went into thinking, talking, and being concerned about matters that did not take place in their actual situation but constituted projections for their future, such as living independently (in whatever way such was visualized), marriage, matters of physical/sexual intimacies, staying home alone and going out alone. Clearly, there were other issues the subjects were preoccupied with that were pertinent to their actual situation (such as work, recreation, health, religion, money, dealing with authority, and interpersonal relations); the point here is that many of the ways the subjects gave meaning to their daily lives dealt with images, concepts, and assumptions about the future, that is, about living conditions that would be different. Also, these particular preoccupations emerged from major categories; that is, these categories account for the greater part of the subjects' behavior.

Following the above reasoning, it would be these images, concepts, and assumptions contained in their projection for the future that define their idea of normalcy.

Preoccupation with the future was not characteristic of subjects of the research by Edgerton (1967), Edgerton and Bercovici (1976), Henshel (1972) and Mattinson (1970). In contrast, most of their energy was spent on their actual situation. The major concerns by Edgerton's (1967) subjects were (1) how to make a living, (2) the proper management of sex, marriage, and reproduction, and (3) the ways in which leisure time could be best utilized. Other studies did not rank the subjects' concerns in order, but the findings show that these concerns were very similar. All subjects of these studies had something in common: they did live independently, that is, they lived without official supervision, and they did have the freedom to marry and be sexually involved.

In sum, the conclusion seems to present itself that normalcy, as defined by what the subjects wanted to be different, meant for most living "on-my-own," coming and going without having to account for it, and the freedom to get married and to be sexually involved. It seems interesting to note that none of the subjects ever expressed the desire to own a house, to have a lot of money, to have a well-paying or stable job or any of the more stereotypic middle class desires. The subjects who did mention money did so only out of concern to have enough to get married or to just live on.

Several other properties were related to the subjects' perceptions of their competence. While they denied being retarded, they were aware of certain limitations and they expressed in different ways their need for other persons. The diagram of this pattern shows these properties and their relations. Below a few examples are offered of observations from which these properties emerged.

Property B: Realizations of one's own limitations (in living skills, academic skills, in knowledge, or emotional maturity).

EXAMPLE 122: In the men's cottage Rob is talking to a relative over the telephone. I hear him say "I could drive a car but they won't let me here." At the end of the conversation he hangs up and the first thing he says is: I am going to get myself a four door . . . get my driver's license. **Houseparent:** Are you working on that in the workshop? **Rob:** Yes, Mr. Brown is helping me. **Author:** What are you learning now? **Rob:** All the signs . . . "it will be a miracle though if I get through." (September 3, visit 45)

EXAMPLE 123: **Pam:** (About marriage) Oh, maybe, but not now. I have my own troubles. I don't want also a husband's troubles. (September 17, visit 51)

Subjects' remarks about their limitations mainly centered around not being able to do academic skills (reading, writing, and math) and not knowing how to do household tasks. Few remarks were made about emotional/psychological limitations. Max volunteered that he would need some supervision when living "alone with Terry" after they would be married, and Pam thought she had enough troubles herself and was not ready to marry, nor to have a baby. Terry realized that she got upset easily.

Perhaps, the subjects' realization of their limitations may be very limited in the eyes of others. The point to be made here is that they did know that there were things they couldn't do.

Property C: Significant others provide guidelines for behavior or act as authority figures.

EXAMPLE 124: Kitty and Terry are calling each other Mrs. and the name of their respective boyfriends. To Jane they say: You are Mrs. – **Jane:** "I am not, I can't marry." **Author:** Why is that Jane? **Jane:** "Well, I can't read, can't write. I can't . . . (could not understand her)." **Lisa:** "With whom have you been?" **Jane:** "With my grandmam." **Lisa:** "Ooooh . . ." **Jane:** My grandmam says that I can't marry as I can't do reading and writing. (September 9, visit 48)

EXAMPLE 125: Don and I are having a lengthy talk about marriage. He tells me that he has the phone number of the girl he has in mind. He then asks: What is your opinion? **Author:** About what? **Don:** About getting married? And a little later: Could I save enough money to get married?

EXAMPLE 126: **Terry:** Terry is telling me that she would not have children . . . "not for a while . . ." **Author:** You told me the other day that you would want a child. Have you changed your mind? **Terry:** Yes, but my mam says that I better not . . . can't do things together . . . it is no fun when you have to take care of a baby. (November 16, visit 69)

EXAMPLE 127: After a lengthy talk with Lisa about the forbidden nature of sexual behavior outside of marriage, she adds: There are two people you have to listen to in your life: God and your mother. (January 21, visit 81)

Property D: Living with significant others or having contact with them (such as weekend visits) is seen as making up for what seems to be lacking in the present situation.

EXAMPLE 128: Lisa is talking about her mother's marriage. Jane says something I can't understand but which makes Lisa upset. I ask what is happening. **Lisa:** She says that my mother should not marry. **Jane:** "You know why?" **Author:** No. **Jane:** "I want my daddy to get back with my mammie so I can live with them again." (October 6, visit 55)

EXAMPLE 129: Terry told me that she and Kitty had had a fight. She had then apologized to Kitty because: "I was in a bad mood. But I told her: 'Kitty, you have a home to go to.'" (November 16, visit 69)

EXAMPLE 130: Rob comes back from a visit home. **Rob:** It is sad to come back here. This is not my home, you know. When I get married, that will be good . . . (September 3, visit 45)

EXAMPLE 131: Lisa and I were talking about her stay at her sister's house over Christmas. I asked her whether she considered her sister's place her home (her sister is her guardian and she spends vacations and some weekends there). **Lisa:** No, not really. **Author:** Is the cottage your home? **Lisa:** That is a "home away from home." You know what I mean? **Author:** Are you saying that it is not a real home to you? **Lisa:** Yes, it is not. She then goes on to say that she would rather live with her mother in an apartment or be married. (January 12, visit 80).

Property E: Significant others are persons who are there when you need them—not having any such persons to turn to is upsetting, depressing, etc.

EXAMPLE 132: Max has been telling me that he wants to "get-out-of-here." I stress that I can't do anything for him. He asks if I am not a psychologist or an analyst. I tell him again what I am here for. **Max:** But who *can* do something for me? (July 10, visit 28)

EXAMPLE 133: Terry was in a crisis situation, throwing a tantrum. She had not been allowed to spend her money the way she wanted while shopping with all of us in the supermarket. I agreed to stay with her in the parking lot where she sobbed and cried. Among other things she said: I want to call Henry (boyfriend at the workshop). I want to go to my mammie and daddie. I can't stand it here. I don't like nobody. Everyone is pushing me around and she is not my boss. No one helps me. I don't care if I get into trouble. I am going away. (August 16, visit 36)

EXAMPLE 134:* Upon entering the cottages, I saw Rob sitting on the little wall outside. He was fiddling around with little sticks, his face was drawn and he did not look right at me. **Author:** Rob, what is the matter? He told me, with his head turned sideways, that he was not allowed to go to church because the houseparent thought he got "too much spirit . . . too much love," and he went on: So, here I am, don't know what to do. I have to figure out what to do (his mouth trembled and he ner-

*In this example the researcher's responses are left out; these responses were merely reactive utterances, such as "Hm," "I see," and "Why?"

vously kept breaking little twigs). I can't go to church anymore; he said I can't go. My mam taught me to follow the path of the Lord. She tried to raise us kids in the right way you know . . . I don't know what way to turn to, so now I am sitting here alone . . . no one to talk to. Oh no, I don't like you to leave, but you can't do anything for me. I can't stand this place . . . want to go and live with my mam. She and I would both go to church, she to hers and I to mine, and then I would come home and wait for her. If you can't live right what is the sense of living . . . I don't know. (August 8, visit 34)

EXAMPLE 135: Don had asked my opinion about getting married and whether I thought he could save enough money (see example 124). **Author:** I don't know these things. I don't know how much they can help you here. **Don:** "Oh . . . they don't have money! (shaking his head). I don't know who can help me. No one has time to help me here!" **Author:** With what? **Don:** "With things." (December 15, visit 71)

Observations of the last property (Property E) came from more or less crisis situations. It seemed that in these kinds of situations, particularly the feeling "no one can help me," occurred. The field notes contained only eight observations of this kind, coming from four subjects (Terry, Rob, Max, and Don).

While eight frequencies is not a high number, it seemed of sufficient importance to include this property because of its theoretical relevance. It shows that persons labeled retarded do have a deep awareness of ultimate helplessness, dependence, and aloneness. Three of the four subjects from which these observations came (Terry, Max, and Rob) were persons who would become upset or depressed easier than the others. It may also be that some similar moods by the noncontributing subjects were missed in the data collection. When the findings of this chapter were presented to houseparents as a validity procedure, they noted the importance of this finding for all subjects. These houseparents mentioned that, especially in crisis situations, everyone but Don had expressed this feeling of ultimate helplessness in one way or another.

The observations under Property E most strongly represented the need for relationships and for help from others, a need which is also found in the observations from which Property C (significant others provide guidelines for behavior) and Property D (significant others make up for what is missing) emerged.

The search for negative cases pointed to Kitty and Don who contributed very little to properties C, D, and E. There seems no explanation for Kitty's absence from these observations within the scope of this research. In a way, Kitty talked a lot, but rarely elaborated upon anything. She would often answer my questions (as well as from others) with a "I forgot now" or "I don't know." Don's lack of contribution may be due to the fact that Don was the only subject who had an intact home. Not only was his family intact, but both parents were very accepting of Don (who was an only child) and appeared to be very caring. Don was a very quiet person, and perhaps he just would not openly express a desire for personal relationships. None of the houseparents could remember having ever heard Don talk about these issues. It may be possible that his stable home base made it unnecessary for him to do so.

An interesting thread ran across many observations from which Property C and D emerged. While authority figures or persons from whom advice was sought included caseworkers, God, staff members, and, on a few occasions, myself, eleven of the twenty-eight observations under Property C (significant others provide guidelines for behavior) refer to a mother (and, in one case, a grandmother). Likewise, eleven of the nineteen observations under Property D (significant others make up for what is missed) make reference to a mother. Jane, Terry, Lisa, and Rob especially referred to their mothers several times and always in a positive manner, accepting the mother's authority or the wish to live with her. The latter was also expressed by Kitty.

Only Pam and Max referred to their mothers in a negative and opposing way. Nevertheless, Pam did see living with her mother as an alternative to living at the cottages, and, at the end of the study, she indeed moved back in with her mother. Max expressed his "hate" for his mother who (according to his perceptions) had been responsible for putting him in a military school, then in a hospital, and had not allowed him to marry a girl in the hospital whom he had loved.

It seemed of interest that not one observation referred to a father alone. Four observations referred to "parents" or "Mommy and Daddy." However, the father of four subjects had passed away (Max, Lisa, Pam, and Rob), which certainly could account for the absence of the father figure. Nevertheless, since there can be various "significant others" in one's life, the data suggest that for most subjects the mother figure elicited strong emotional/psychological reactions. Abel and Kinder (1949), who describe something of the substance of the lives of eighty adolescent girls who were being given industrial training in New York City, similarly noted the importance given to the mother figure.

Table VIII shows that 89 percent of the statements indicating the importance of other persons was volunteered. This pattern does *not* include any of the 158 observations indicating the need for others within the marriage and boy/girl friend relationship (see Chapter 4): these needs included the need for companionship, the need to be cared for and to be loved, the need for someone to be physically involved with, for someone to talk to, to be understood by, and the need for someone with whom to enter into a relationship that suggested some permanency for the future. Thus, besides the 55 observations in the present pattern indicating the need for significant others, there were 158 observations that noted a need for others with specific regard to boy/girl friend relations and to marriage. In sum, it is patent that relationships with others were invested with a great deal of meaning. Other persons were much needed to make sense out of living.

Discussion

It has been hypothesized by many that being labeled directly affects self-concept, learning, and performance and that the effects may be lifelong (Blatt, 1972; Dunn, 1968; Jones, 1972). MacMillan, Jones, and Aloia (1974) note that such a view has apparently been unchallenged as one reads the accounts of litigations charging, in part, that the labeling of the child as mentally retarded has devastating and long-lasting effects; however, as these authors note, no empirical evidence to support such hypotheses has been found.

Hypothesizing a pure effect of the label retarded assumes that the label can be separated from its consequences. Conceptually, one can do this, and researchers do so when designing research in an attempt to measure the effect of the label. Professionals do so when assigning labels to persons and subsequently choosing from various possible actions that then become the consequence of the label. However, the data of the present study, as well as other naturalistic studies referred to earlier, suggest that for the persons at the receiving end of the labeling process, such separation may be extremely difficult to perceive or may not exist at all. When asked, the subjects of the present study denied the appropriateness of the label 'retarded' for them, though most were not able to define what it meant. Their spontaneous, voluntary reactions to their retarded status were in terms of the actual specific consequences of the label, and the same observation can be made for the subjects of the other studies referred to. Rationalizations for being in a place for the retarded were explanations for having been subjected to the particular placement.

The possibility that may exist is that the separation of label and consequence exists for the researcher, the theorist, or the professional, but not for the receiver. For the receiver, label and consequence are one: either the consequence experienced personally, or the observed consequence for someone else. Several examples from the literature would seem to support this notion. For instance, the subject of an intensive interview (Bogdan and Taylor, 1976) made the following statement:

> It's funny. You hear so many people talking about IQ. The first time I ever heard the expression was when I was at Empire State School. I didn't know what it was or anything, but some people were talking and they brought the subject up. It was on the ward, and I went and asked one of the staff what mine was. They told me 49. Forty-nine isn't fifty, but I was pretty happy about it. I mean I figured that I wasn't a low grade. I really didn't know what it meant, but it sounded pretty high. Hell, I was born in 1948 and forty-nine didn't seem too bad. Forty-nine didn't sound hopeless. I didn't know anything about the highs or the lows, but I knew I was better than most of them.

The label "IQ 49" did not have a negative effect, in fact it sounded quite good. However, Ed did mind being institutionalized; he simply was not aware of the connection between the "IQ 49" label and the consequences of the label—his institutionalization.

Mattinson (1970, p. 62) faced total objection by her subjects when she requested to test their children. They said: "I remember those tests. I went into the hospital after them, I'm not having my Rosie put away. She is all right. You leave us alone." It seems that rather than fearing the stigma of low intelligence, they feared a behavioral consequence. On the other hand, Henshel (1972, p. 216 and 228) found that the 33 percent of the subjects who had children who were also judged retarded were "amazingly tolerant" of their children's retardation and showed a "moving acceptance." There was no fear that anything would happen to their children by acknowledging their retardation. The important difference between Mattinson's and Henshel's subjects, in terms of support for the perception of oneness of label and consequence by the receiver, is that the former persons had been institutionalized while the latter never had been.

In 1967, Edgerton's subjects initially reacted with suspicion and fear of reinstitutionalization. Their efforts at concealment of their retarded status often took the shape of concealing that they had been in the institution. Again and again, the words "I never belonged there in the first place" were recorded; "These subjects saw their release from the institution as a confirmation of the error of the original diagnosis of mental retardation that had sent them there . . ." (Edgerton, 1967, p. 147). It is clear that for these persons the consequence and the label were perceived as one.

In 1976, as years of living in the community had past, the concern by Edgerton's subjects about the label retarded had reduced considerably—and no fear was expressed about the possibility of reinstitutionalization. It seemed that the effect of the label had been maintained, or not maintained, in terms of the nature of its continuing consequences or of the absence of such consequences.

An example taken from MacMillan et al. (1974) may also serve to hypothesize the inherent oneness of label and consequence for the receiver of the label. MacMillan et al. state:

> The impact of being labeled mentally retarded varies tremendously from individual to individual, depending on circumstances. At the extremes the label probably has no effect whatsoever. For example, a very bright adolescent with a history of academic success would shrug off such a label and an institutionalized hydrocephalic with IQ< 10 would not be able to comprehend the significance of being labeled retarded (p. 253).

The terms "depending on circumstances," "shrug off," and "the significance of the label" essentially have to do with the consequences of the label. The persons with IQ<10 would not be able to understand the significance of the label because s/he would not see the connection with its consequences. Thus, the label may indeed not mean anything. However, the consequences may. For all we know, such persons may not like being institutionalized. The bright adolescent can afford to shrug off the label precisely because it does not have any consequences. If one would be put in an institution regardless, one would mind the label.

Edgerton and Sabagh (1962) suggest that it may be crucial for the person in an institution to deny the label retarded in order to succeed in being released from the institution and to succeed in adjusting to community living. Acceptance of the label retarded was seen as submission to custodial care in the institution. These suggestions clearly reflect the oneness of label and consequence for the receiver of the label.

From these examples it seems warranted to suggest that the label has an effect on the receiver only after the connection with its consequences has been perceived and in terms of these consequences. If the notion of oneness of label and consequences holds, research investigating a pure effect of the label would lose its meaning. Investigating the effect of the label would necessarily mean investigation of the effects of the particular consequences for particular persons in their particular settings.

Another comparison between findings of the present study and other studies referred to deals with the need for personal relationships. Subjects of this study showed a great need for significant others to help them, advise them, and provide them with a homelike atmosphere. For Edgerton's (1967) subjects, it was critical to have normal benefactors (relatives, landlords, bosses). Henshel

(1972) also notes the supportive network of relatives that made life easier, especially for the Chicano subjects. Interestingly, in 1976 (Edgerton and Bercovici) the need for benefactors had decreased considerably. For the married persons, the need for friendships and companionship was often met by the spouse (see Chapter 4). The passage of time had brought successful community adjustment for most and the need for benefactors had diminished. Other researchers have also observed that most persons whom we label retarded and who live in the community adjust satisfactorily, but such adjustment typically does take time (see Edgerton and Bercovici, 1976, and MacMillan et al., 1974).

Passage of time means, in fact, experience in living in the actual behavioral setting to which one is to adjust. The need for time, that is, for living experience in the actual situation, has implications: to wait till subjects "are ready" would be contradictory to reality. "Readiness" may not be a measureable state of achievement, a prerequisite, but rather a process which evolves in the setting to which one is to adjust. From this perspective, readiness cannot be judged outside of such setting. This may be one factor why prediction of community adjustment has been so unreliable (see Edgerton and Bercovici, 1976, for a discussion of the unreliability of community adjustment prediction). Mattinson (1970, p. 198) found no correlation between IQ and adjustment to living as a married couple outside of the institution:

> Perhaps then the key to whether a particular patient is likely to succeed or not in his marriage, depends not so much on the actual level of intelligence, nor on the actual circumstances of his deprivation, but more on his motivation to succeed and on his ability to relate to a member of the opposite sex, using that relationship to overcome or to accept his own disability and to withstand or contain both his own and his partner's strength of feeling. Prediction and professional help may then have to be concerned more with these two factors: motivation and the ability to relate over time.

The motivation "to make it" is a reoccurring theme by all subjects of the studies referred to, and many do—in spite of negative predictions and attitudes by professionals and laypersons alike, or, as Meyers (1978, p. 100), who lived with his subject (his retarded brother) for years, states it: in spite of "the ignorance, arrogance, and stupidity of others."

It seemed patent that once one has been labeled retarded, the most important thing in life becomes to show that one *can* manage one's own affairs. The subjects of the present study also clearly expressed their motivation and their confidence that they could make it on their own (Chapter 3). This determination "to make it" was concisely expressed by Rob, in discussing marriage:

> **Rob:** We will be living together, have our own place. I'll take her out to supper and to the movies. I'll do anything: get up at five . . . four . . . any time. **Author:** To work, you mean? **Rob:** Yes. (May 23, visit 2)

Mattinson (1970) suggests that motivation and the ability to relate to each other was responsible for the successful adjustment to independent life as a married couple, rather than intelligence and particular circumstances. Edgerton and Bercovici (1976) however, found the particular circumstances to play an important and sometimes decisive role. Public attitudes, welfare legislation, employment opportunities, death of spouse, or divorce were all found to have had significant impact on adjustment, either positively or negatively. These authors also point to the greater vulnerability to shifting and unexpected circumstances by the less competent. They do not have resources to fall back on as do more competent persons.

In sum, while persons we label retarded and who live in supervised settings (as the subjects of the present study) need benefactors and many significant others, this is not to say that such needs reduce the chances for future adjustment to independent living. The literature suggests that the actual experience in independent living may reduce the need for help from benefactors. Judgment of readiness, by preconceived criteria (such as measurements of personality, attitude, independence, intelligence, or vocational skills) may or may not relate to later adjustment. The strength of the motivation to make it and the determination to manage one's own affairs may be a more accurate predictor. Particular circumstances (job market, welfare, divorce, death) are difficult to predict, but it may be with regard to such circumstances that professional help may be needed most. If the findings on community adjustment noted above hold, judgments of readiness for persons such as the subjects in the present study lose much of their assumed meaning. It would then follow that professionals would be more effective in facilitation of successful living for these persons if we do what Guskin (in Rhodes, 1975) suggests: find out what the less competent person's needs are and provide alternatives from which they could choose. What they wish for is not all that much.

The literature, and the present study, shows that they want a rather simple life, as long as they can show themselves, and thus the world, that they can manage their own daily affairs either with or without socially acceptable ways of assistance. After having been judged incompetent to do so, that appears to be a most crucial ingredient to meaningful living.

Chapter 7

SUMMARY AND CONCLUSIONS

THE FOREGOING has been an attempt to reconstruct some of the ways in which persons placed in a group home for the retarded experienced meaning, or lack of meaning, in their lives. The essential attitude behind this research was: given our concern about the quality of life for the less competent in our care, we need to know how *they* view life as meaningful so we can assist them with the skills we have and they lack, to live the kinds of lives they want to live. Thus, the practicality of the kind of knowledge rendered by this study is twofold. As was noted in Chapter 1, insight in the ways other persons construct reality may clarify communication. Second, while this knowledge does not render specific guidelines, rules, or know-how for program planning and implementation, it does offer a data base from which such specific guidelines for specific situations can emerge.

BOUNDARIES OF THE STUDY

It may be the case that the findings of this study have a good deal of generalizability, since the major characteristics of the setting are rather representative of the general philosophy of program planning and implementation for the less competent adult in North America. However, in different settings and geographical locations, a study like the present one may find additional or modified findings of the ways less competent persons in various settings view meaning in their lives. Also, different researchers may observe more or fewer events, may establish a different rapport with the subjects, which may elicit different data, may see patterns in the data that varied from the ones isolated here, or may attach different importance to the findings; rather than an indication of subjectiveness of the data, this would merely indicate the complexity of human behavior, social settings, and their interaction. Validity is not a matter of offering all that there is to offer, but rather a matter of securing that what is offered was indeed there. Naturalistic procedures do not break down all deception, nor do they reduce the complexities of human life to a clear and simple truth. As Edgerton (1975) stresses, the method is not intended to provide simple answers; it is intended to provide empirical grounds for rejecting simple answers in favor of fuller and more accurate understanding of human behavior.

The data of this study may well constitute the most obvious of all behavioral patterns since this study was a first attempt to investigate how persons in a group home saw themselves and their lives. The study could not build upon previous findings. Nevertheless, the isolated patterns seemed to indicate major areas of concern and accounted for the greater part of the subjects' behavior. The field notes do include other categories of behavioral events that could not be sufficiently investigated within the scope of this study to warrant presentation of distinct findings. These categories dealt with subjects' perceptions of their health, religion, recreation, sex roles, and certain aspects of work and money. Future research may find these aspects—and undoubtedly others as well—fertile ground for investigation to obtain a more fully integrated picture of how less competent persons in supervised settings in this culture see meaning, or lack of meaning, in their lives.

The remainder of this chapter will first summarize the findings and subsequently suggest some thoughts for possible directions for research and program planning.

SUBJECTS' PERSPECTIVE ON MEANING: A SUMMARY

While the previous chapters discussed the data of this study in professional phraseology, this summary will note the findings as if spoken by the subjects. Clearly, no subject expressed ways in which s/he saw life as meaningful in a cummulative narrative, though many of the phrases noted below were actually said. The purpose of summarizing the data in this manner is to emphasize the aim of this research: to grasp some of the ways in which meaning was given to living. One way to do so is to state the findings as these persons might if they could deliberately and reflectively step out of their reality.

On independence

We badly want to be more independent than we can be here. We want to be able to stay home alone, go out by ourselves, and we feel good when we can spend money the way we want. It also feels good to own a lot of things, things that other people use. Owning a car or just to be able to drive would make some of us feel very independent. Some of us want a job in the community, but we all want to get out of here, not so much because we don't like it here (although sometimes we don't) but we just want to be on-our-own. We can't stand having to listen to others all the time, sometimes even to people much younger than we are. We don't like being told what to do. Always being with other people, that gets to be a hassle too. We think we are capable of living on our own, with a little help here or there, but that's all right. Everyone needs help sometimes. We want to live alone or with a roommate or marry and be on our own.

On marriage, physical/sexual involvement, having children, and boy/girl friend relationships

We want to get married, and most of us will, soon, or in a few years. Some day we will, because it brings the things we want. It will give us a home, companionship, and care, but especially, it will take us out of here and then we can be on our own. It will also allow us to be involved in sexual behavior, and that must be very exciting.

I do know about sexual behavior that involves more than holding hands or giving a kiss, and I'll engage in it when I'm married, including having sex. I can't have all this yet, as it belongs in marriage (especially intercourse, that would be bad to do now), but it does sound exciting, and, actually, I can't wait till I am married so I can find out more about it.

Clearly, our boy/girl friends also know about all this and find it exciting and that makes us use it as a tease sometimes and as a challenge or a promise. We refer to it a lot when we are all together, make remarks when we see things on television or in the movies, and we joke about it. However, it is a topic that one does not easily talk seriously about, and not with the staff. I hardly would dare to mention it. After all, they forbid us to do it now and no one talks openly about it. We kind of have to pick up knowledge about sex ourselves where we can.

We do feel somewhat tense and anxious about it, though. It is all rather confusing. We can't do it, yet we get all the messages about how exciting it must be. The television tells us so, the movies, pictures in books, remarks made by staff, words in songs we hear. It must be an important thing in life. But we can't have it; one must be married and we cannot marry here. Thus it is normal for us that we can't engage in it. We must not be ready for it.

Of course, we can be somewhat intimate with our boy/girl friends. We can sit close, kiss, hold hands, and even sneak in a tight hug or embrace. That is fun and exciting, but it leads us to desire more of it. It makes us feel a little nervous or uneasy, too. It all seems exciting and we find ourselves teasing others with the idea of marriage. Oh, yes, we'll have children, more than one perhaps, when we are married. We can take care of them, but it is not all that important right now. We think of marriage and sex much more than of having children.

One way to get married is to start with having a boy/girl friend. It is very important to us to have a boy/girl friend. In fact, for most of us, it is so important that we will take anyone who is available, of course, if possible the one we like best. A boy/girl friend belongs to you, and you to him/her, so you must kind of watch out for others who may try and take her/him away.

To have a boy/girl friend is nice right now, too. For some of us it means having someone to show off and talk about, for others it is important to have someone close to talk to, to feel understood by, someone who listens to you and for whom you can care. For some of us it is important that s/he gives you things, or helps you decide what to do.

For all of us, to have a boy/girl friend strengthens the idea that marriage is really possible and that one day we will get out of here. If our present boy/girl friend leaves, we will take another one, for it is important to keep believing that we, too, can marry and live on our own one day, and do the things we want to do, just as everyone else.

On interpersonal understanding

We do often understand quite a bit about other persons' behavior and their situations. When we are on good terms with a person or when we are in a good mood, we use that knowledge to give advice, to help, or to show concern. At other times we can use what we know to get something out of it for ourselves. There are also times that we like to tell others what to do and boss them around. Sometimes it works; sometimes it does not, but it mostly seems to work with the people here who can't talk back and who don't know how to boss *us* around. It feels very good to have such power.

There are also persons about whom we don't know much. We like to find out things about them that interest us or are puzzling, especially when it is different from the way we live.

On intrapersonal understanding

We know that we are in a place for "the retarded" and we know there are things we cannot do (such as reading, writing, cooking good things, and math) but that does not make us retarded. We are not sure what the word exactly means but it must be something very bad because when we call each other retarded we can be fired from our job. We have heard that that has happened. But, yes, . . . we are here . . . but you see, most of us have reasons for being here (which is not the same as being retarded, to be sure), such as having parents who do not want us, a mother who always fights; some of us have seizures and, therefore, could not be home alone, or some would be lonely at home without peers. Some of us, to tell you the truth, cannot quite figure out why we are here. So, we are not retarded: we are normal. But we are not living like most people do. It is confusing to figure all this out. Most of us have a hard time putting in words what being normal means, but we do know that we want to live differently from the way we do now. We do want to be on our own, but we already told you all about that. It may be difficult to live alone, but with someone else we probably can manage. That's one reason why most of us want to marry. We know that we need help right now already. We need people to tell us what to do and make a home for us. Some of us think of our mothers when we feel that way. Sometimes things get tough or lonely around here and it is very upsetting and depressing when there is no one to turn to and to depend on. Then you really feel how terribly alone you stand in this world. Then we feel how dependent we really are. We need to keep believing that we have some say over our lives and that, one day, we will be able to make our own decisions, just as other people do.

THOUGHTS ON DIRECTIONS FOR RESEARCH AND PROGRAM PLANNING

To view the following thoughts on directions for research and program planning as relevant, the reader needs to share the attitudinal framework behind this study: we are concerned about the quality of life of the persons we label retarded, and the judgment of quality is primarily their judgment and not ours.

This attitude has been more poetically expressed by Albert Camus:* "If you want the happiness of the people, let them speak out and tell what kind of happiness they want and what kind they don't want."

Without this attitude most program planning and research will necessarily continue to reflect *our* ways of giving meaning to living and *our* thoughts about appropriate ways of living for the persons in our care. As Edgerton and Bercovici (1976, p. 495) have characterized the predominant professional attitude: "*We,* after all, have been responsible for *them.*" It appears that in several major ways, our decisions have been directing their lives away from meaningful living as defined by them, specifically with regard to the meaning of work, normalization, marriage, and sex-

*Quoted by Biklen, in the Politics of Institutions, in B. Blatt, D. Biklen, and R. Bogden (Eds.) *An Alternative Textbook in Special Education,* Love Publishing Company, 1977, p. 29.

ual involvement.

When focusing on the quality of life as judged by the persons who do the living, several implications for research are apparent. First, investigations of ways in which meaning is given to life by the less competent in various settings need to be an inherent and ongoing part of research investigating the construct of mental retardation. It needs to be ongoing as changes in behavioral settings and socioeconomic and technological changes in society at large may bring about changes in the way sense is made out of life.

Second, it would seem important to investigate *how* these ways of giving meaning are being shaped. That is, what particular aspects of the setting impact upon the ways these persons come to view their reality as orderly? For instance, the data discussed in Chapter 4 of this study alluded to a possible connection between the strict rules against sexual involvement in the group home setting and the subjects' insistence on placing sexual involvement within the marriage context. The data in Chapter 5 suggested possible influence of extensive television watching within the rather isolated environment of the group home.

A third implication would concern studies of community adjustment. Criteria, typically used in debates about adequate or inadequate adjustment, such as income and job stability, would continue to be of interest for factual information but cannot be taken as sole indices of the quality of life. For instance, the emphasis on the dignity of work and economic independence, which is pervasive in normalization principles, is not necessarily shared to the same extent by the persons being normalized. The data of this study and the existing literature indicate that work is mainly seen as a means to earn a living and that other means are quite acceptable. Married life, sexual expression, friends, and leisure time are in most cases judged to be far more important. As Edgerton and Bercovici (1976, p. 493) note: "They can learn to do without work rather nicely . . ." This is not at all to suggest that work cannot bring dignity or cannot increase the quality of life, but that it does not do so by the mere fact of being work.

Another area of concern would regard administrative placement and transfer decisions. Having friends and relationships with other persons was exceedingly important for the subjects of this study as well as for most of the subjects of the studies to which reference has been frequently made. Friendships and relationships provided fulfillment of daily needs, but also provided a sense of security, stability, and continuation of the flow of events in one's life. Having friends and relationships, without doubt, is also highly important for most of us. However, most of us lack experience of what it means to have *no* control over one's life, no freedom to live where one wants to live, to see whom one wants to see, to phone whom one wants to phone. We are free persons in the sense that we have free access to friends, can see them, phone them, drive or fly to them, and have the skills to write them—and most of us take all of these freedoms for granted. Yet, it is an important way of giving meaning to life, the extent of which we may only become aware of when, for whatever reason, we find ourselves cut off from our friends. It is then that we experience that we took "having friends" for granted. As Hall (1959, 1973) notes, it is often the most obvious in one's cultural setting that is lost to awareness in observation. It may be that this out-of-awareness nature of the importance of friendship is partially responsible for many placement decisions by administrators of institutions and group homes that do not take into account these persons' friendships. Bureaucratic decisions may break up relationships that may have been one of the very few sources of security and sense of continuity for the persons involved.

The foregoing is to strongly suggest that awareness of our own ways of giving meaning to our lives is crucial, so that the taken-for-granted and out-of-awareness notions that guide us do not prevent us from seeing what is needed or what may be critical in helping the less competent to increase the quality of their lives.

One way to increase awareness of our own ways of making sense of life is to expose ourselves to the ways of other cultures. Hall (1959, p. 30) states that one of the most effective ways to learn about oneself is by taking seriously the cultures of others:

> Years of study have convinced me that the real job is not to understand foreign culture but to understand our own. I am also convinced that all that one ever gets from studying foreign culture is a token understanding. The ultimate reason for such study is to learn more about how one's own system works. The best reason for expos-

> ing oneself to foreign ways is to generate a sense of vitality and awareness – an interest in life which can come only when one lives through the shock of contrast and difference.

It is indeed the lack of awareness of other cultural modes of thoughts that cause the risk of being culture bound (Smith, 1978).

How exposure to ways in which other cultures implement programs for their less competent citizens can increase awareness of the ways we go about doing so is pointedly illustrated by Wolfensberger (1972; 1977). After describing the way the Scandinavian culture deals with sexuality for the less competent citizens in supervised settings (where sexual relations are allowed and marriage is facilitated), Wolfensberger (1972, p. 166) states: "I freely admit that these discoveries (in early 1969), as well as the matter-of-fact way they were viewed and communicated to me, shook me up." As a result of this shock, Wolfensberger continues to explore why, in North America, sexuality for the retarded and the impaired makes us uncomfortable. Without the Scandinavian exposure, the subsequent reflection may not have occurred.

In 1977, Wolfensberger (p. 335) similarly remarks on "the challenge of the Scandinavian experience" with regard to the vast differences in activation processes. Wolfensberger learned that approximately five times as many movement-impaired retarded persons were "bed-lyers" in North America as compared with Scandinavia. The question then presented itself: "Why do we have so many people who see no alternatives to our current practices?" (Wolfensberger, 1977, p. 337).

When we listen more clearly to what the less competent tell us they want from their lives, it appears not to be all that much: a rather simple life with no high expectations of any particular kind. It would be one in which they can show that they may have the abilities to make it on their own, according to their own values, and for most, preferably within a marriage context from which they can derive a sense of home and companionship, and use their combined strengths to manage the tasks required in day-to-day living. Having a job and earning money is seen as subservient to these goals. This is not to say that these persons would not want to have more money, a house, a car, but that they set other priorities. It may well be our own priorities that prevent us from understanding theirs, which are typically of no concern to us: we have them and take them for granted as a minimum base for living.

It appears that help from professionals, from relatives, and from welfare agencies is not perceived as a stigma of incompetence. Rather, the stigma of incompetence is connected with placement in a supervised setting where one cannot make one's own decisions.

The question arises: when are these persons ready to live the way they want to live, and how do we know? It may be that this is the wrong question to ask. In Chapter 6 it was noted that readiness, as usually defined by criteria of IQ, vocational skills, or demonstrated competence, has not been reliably related to successful adjustment, whether judged by researchers or by the persons who did the adjusting. Many other unknown variables and life's circumstances may account for adjustment, or lack of it. It appears that the strength of the motivation to make it, the availability of benefactors and assistance, and particular circumstances (death of spouse, divorce, availability, and social acceptability of welfare) may bear more directly on a person's adjustment.

Our professional challenge may be to find out how we can assist them in the actual process of living the way they desire. Guskin (in Rhodes, 1975) suggested some years ago that perhaps it should be the task of the parents and the child to decide what they want and need, and the task of the professional to provide alternatives from which they can choose. As the less competent person grows up, the issue becomes more urgent still. As Hobbs (1975, p. 117) states, the older person is held legally accountable for his actions, and s/he, in fact, becomes the best judge of how his or her life should be lived.

Rather than a "waiting till ready" philosophy of programming, the above notions could lead to a "trying out" philosophy, which could incorporate a swinging door concept, where flexibility exists to go back to a more supervised setting when needed. An ideal situation, some may say, but it may be a far more realistic one. In fact, the readiness/prediction paradigm appears to be an ideal state of affairs, which has not in any consistent way related to reality.

For as long as the less competent are in supervised settings, the literature and the data of the present study urge consideration of extending the limits of independence wherever possible. In many situations it must be possible to allow clients greater independence, to allow them to stay home alone for certain periods of time, to go out unsupervised, to date, to arrange their rooms the way they want (with or without junk), to allow free use of the telephone, to allow money to be spent without having to account for it, and to provide opportunities for privacy and solitude. All these aspects are symbols of normalcy, which do not have to be taken away from them—even if doing so would be more convenient, would be more in accordance with the ways staff members give meaning to their own living, or would fit staff members perceptions of how the residents should live.

The foregoing discussion leads to a central question. If we indeed are serious about normalization principles and increasing the quality of life of the less competent persons in our care, we have to ask ourselves: What has kept us from allowing these persons to live the way they want to live? Besides the possible distorting effect of our perceptions of meaning for our own lives, one answer to this question points to the issues of marriage, sexuality, and child rearing.

Given the fact that marriage is seen as possible and valuable by the persons we label retarded and, indeed, appears to be a viable alternative for them, research needs to investigate why marriage has not been facilitated by mental retardation professionals (either before or after acceptance of normalization principals). A cross-cultural comparison by Wolfensberger (1972, p. 165) illustrates that different arrangements are possible:

> Early during my trip, in Copenhagen, I visited one of the finest hostels for mildly to moderately retarded young adult women that I have ever seen. There I learned that as the 14 residents in this hostel are socialized into the culture and into adulthood, they are also socialized into 'normal' i.e. culturally normative, sexual patterns.
>
> For instance, as these young women learn to date and relate to male peers, they may become very attached to a young man; in time, the young couple may decide to have sexual relations, and the girl may ask the housemother for contraceptive guidance. The housemother sees to it that the girl will be counseled, and if her intent is

> confirmed, she may be given a choice such as between the pill, an intrauterine device, or voluntary sterilization. In time, she may go to live with the young man, and the national retardation service system may provide the couple with an apartment. Eventually, she may marry. The woman might not have children, but the fact that she is married, or lives with a man, or engages in a socio-sexual relationship, does not faze the retardation service system, which continues to provide services to her. In other words, where a Canadian or American housemother might admonish one of her date-bound retarded girls to "be good", the Scandinavian housemother is more apt to remind her to "be safe", to know her own mind, and to make her decisions strong ones.

This cultural comparison poses the question why marriage and sexuality have not been facilitated in North America while there is no evidence that these expressions in life by less competent persons are less adjusted than those by their fellow citizens of equal economic background. If anything, adjustment may be better (Mattinson, 1970). A related finding comes from Abelson and Johnson (1969), Gunzberg (1968), and from Money (1973): residents who were sexually active were found less aggressive and better adjusted than those who were not.

To facilitate expression of sexuality and marriage, program planning and implementation would have to include open communication about sexuality: complete sex education including discussions of lovemaking, contraceptives, sterilization, childbearing, and childrearing (see also Gordon, 1977, and Edgerton, 1973). Discussions would need to be accompanied by opportunities for normal dating, an activity that now is to be typically done in secrecy.

Child rearing has been found to be a particularly heavy burden for less competent persons. However, several of these persons, if not most, may want to be a parent once married and may view being a parent as a symbol of normalcy. Edgerton (1973) is the first to my knowledge to suggest providing these persons with opportunities to serve as surrogate parents. This could be done in cooperation with school systems, children's wards in hospitals, day care centers, and homes.

Experience in parenting may on one hand satisfy needs and enhance self-esteem, and at the other hand provide realistic experiences that may help to understand the difficulties involved in child rearing. The surrogate parent may also come to understand (and be informed of) the fact that child rearing is difficult for many unlabeled parents as well, and that many people in society at large choose not to have children. Such experiences, combined with a comprehensive sex education, including the facts of sterilization, may well lead to the choice of sterilization as a method of birth control. However, this issue clearly stays a complex one. Sterilization traditionally implies a judgment of incompetence. For persons who deny the label of incompetence (the label retarded) the idea of sterilization may never become popular. On the other hand, if the person understands that sterilization can facilitate independent living, marriage, and sexual involvement (thus actually reducing the total stigma of incompetence) it may appear to be a sensible choice. Such possibility is suggested by Money (1973, p. 5) :

> I have interviewed retarded people who are managing to live at home but who would not be able to look after children, or would run the risk of transmitting a genetic disease if they reproduced. I have found that when they understand these issues they usually decide in favor of sterilization so that they can accept the possibility of romance and sexuality in their adult lives.

Several subjects in Henshel's (1972) study choose sterilization. Meyer's (1978) account of his retarded brother and wife likewise describes the process of counseling and weighing the pro's and con's of rearing children, leading to the couple's decision not to have any. The husband, who particularly wanted children, then decided to pursue a job as an aide in a child-care center.

While mandatory sterilization has been found to be a devastating experience for most (Edgerton, 1967), the chances are far higher that voluntary sterilization may be less damaging or may even be perceived as beneficial.

It has been suggested by several readers of this study that the behavioral patterns it isolates are also characteristic of adolescents in our culture. Indeed, the resistence to supervision, the desire to be more independent, the excessive talk about boy friends and girl friends, the tease and challenge involved in physical contact and references to marriage—all are recognizable in common experience. The harm in this analogy lies in the implication that the responsibility for adolescentlike behavior rests upon the persons we place in these supervised settings. This may not be so. Second, the characteristics of the settings in which adolescents live and the more strictly supervised settings for "the retarded" differ greatly in their supervisory structure, although they may appear similar. Third, the analogy provides another label, one which has a condescending notion for an adult person.

Rather than stating that these persons behave much like adolescents, it seems more accurate to conclude that we, by constructing the settings in which we place them, are at least partially responsible for their adolescentlike behaviors. In settings in which the extent and nature of supervision is similar to the setting of the present study, the residents may have no other option. The questions to ask ourselves would seem to be the following: how can a setting with twenty-four hour supervision, in which one needs to account for all time spent outside of the setting and where one has to obey a variety of persons often younger than oneself, with no more physical contact allowed than holding hands and sitting close, with little or no sex education or open communication about sexuality, with no opportunity for normal dating or for privacy with a person of the opposite sex, and with no facilitation or serious discussion of marriage—how can a setting like this possibly elicit normal adult behavior? Besides expressing oneself through behaviors the setting does allow (and which resemble adolescentlike behaviors) the only option would appear to be to deny desire for independence and sexual expression all together. Also, the group home setting differed in distinct ways from the typical setting in which adolescents live. Adolescents have many unsupervised hours in their lives. They know that supervision will become less and less and will come to a stop in a matter of years. In addition, supervision normally comes from parents who are older and who, at least according to the ways of our culture, have some natural right to authority.

The notion that behavior results from the interaction between the person and her/his environment has become a dictum. Adolescentlike behaviors by adult persons in a strictly supervised setting may be a function of both a delay in their development and the particular constraints we place on them.

Analogies, as cultural comparisons, can be excellent devices to become aware of the reasons why we do what we do. The analogy between adolescentlike behaviors and the behavioral patterns isolated in this study can make us aware of the possibility that we may at least be partially responsible for the occurrence of these behaviors by adult persons in strictly supervised settings. This may prompt an approach to programming more conducive to socialization into normal adult living patterns. However small the evidence in the United States may be at present, it shows that given timely and needed help, many of the less competent persons we placed in institutions or supervised settings are capable of living the kind of lives they define as meaningful while doing no harm to themselves or others. The freedom to choose their own life-styles is not only their natural right, but it also provides professionals with guidelines to effectively assist them with the competencies we have and they do not. To further investigate the specifics of how this can be done on a larger scale is beyond a doubt a major, a meaningful, and a most urgent task.

Appendix A

DESCRIPTION OF SUBJECTS

Terry is an eighteen year old female, who is a ward of the court. Terry does not know her parents, which was a major source of self-pity for her. Her need for a home, for friends, and for boyfriends was expressed over and over.

Terry is rather heavy set and often complained about aches and "not feeling well." She could be rather moody, but at other times very lively and spontaneous.

At the beginning of the research Terry attended special education classes located within the workshop facilities. Later, she was transfered to the workshop where she sorted zippers.

Terry was never institutionalized. Her psychological reports included the labels "TMR functioning level," "Moderately retarded," but with "No physical defect or abnormality." IQ scores and subscores ranged from 45 to 72.

Kitty is a twenty-four year old female, who comes from a poor family background, characterized by alcoholism and physical/sexual abuse. Kitty has a three year old child, who was given up for adoption. Kitty's appearance and way of dress could be described as fitting stereotypes of lower working class persons.

Kitty's verbal expression was rather fragmentary. She spoke in very short sentences and rarely expressed either personal needs or feelings. She often answered questions with a "I don't know," or "I forgot now."

Psychological reports mentioned "generalized retardation," and "TMR functioning level." IQ scores and subscores ranged from 41 to 49. For five years, Kitty had been breaking glass at the recycling plant, which requires considerable safety procedures.

She was said to be a "hard, dependable worker" and was seen by staff members as perhaps capable of living on her own at some point in the future.

Pam is a nineteen year old rather pale and sullen looking female, who used to be obese but now appeared rather attractive. She dressed neatly and when I met her the first time I thought she was a volunteer. Pam is one of six children. Her father died some years ago and she never got along with her mother. As a teenager, Pam was placed in TMR classes where she functioned well and EMR classes were subsequently suggested. She went to the state hospital where she was admitted because of "epilepsy, mental retardation, and behavioral reaction." IQ scores and subscores ranged from 67 to 91.

In the group home Pam was a loner. She spent much time in her room where she watched TV, listened to the radio, or embroidered. She often complained about the nuisance of being with other people.

Pam was on medication for seizure control as well as on tranquilizers.

Lisa is a thirty-eight year old female, with a congenital genetic defect, who would occasionally experience seizures. She used to be obese, but now was almost thin. Lisa lived with her sister before coming to the cottages. Her father died when she was a child. Her mother experienced a stroke and was also a client at the workshop during the time of the research.

Lisa showed a pleasant personality; she loved to "mother" others and was very talkative. She had an excellent vocabulary. Psychological reports noted IQ scores and subscores from 47 to 80, and contained the diagnosis "mental defective." Houseparents judged Lisa to be able to live with greater independence. Her major problem was noted to be her forgetfulness and her self-concept: she thinks she needs help where she does not. Lisa had been sorting paper at the recycling plant for three years. Towards the end of the research she was transferred to vocational rehabilitation where she started sorting zippers. Lisa was on medication for seizure control as well as on tranquilizers.

Jane is a rather small, heavy-set nineteen year old female, who loved to touch and be affectionate with people. She dressed neatly and was characterized as a clean housekeeper and a well organized worker. She had worked in the recycling plant, sorting paper, for several years.

Jane had a speech problem, and also exhibited "baby talk" especially when returning from visits to her mother and grandmother. Her psychological reports noted IQ scores and subscores between 47 and 65. Jane attended one year of special education classes and spent two brief periods in a state school, before coming to the workshop. Jane is on medication for seizure control.

Rob is a nineteen year old male, who was a victim of RH factor. He attended special education classes. Psychological reports noted the labels "moderately retarded" and "slow learner," and TMR classes were suggested. IQ scores and subscores ranged form 43 to 71.

Rob is an avid church attender (three times a week), for which occasions he always dressed very neatly. He played the organ rather well, showed leadership talents, and was characterized by the houseparents as a very sophisticated manipulator. While most subjects used their free time watching television, Rob displayed a variety of interests: he liked to play his records and the radio, and took every chance to go out into the community. He seemed to know his way around and showed himself to be a rather competent roller skater, horse rider, and bowler. He also obtained a CB license and said he was studying for a driver's license.

Rob's major problem was said to be his sexuality, which he directed towards younger children—although his expressed thoughts and projections much referred to women and marriage. Rob was considered by most staff-members capable of living independently.

Don, a twenty-nine year old male, is an only child and comes from an accepting and caring family. Don always seemed healthy and ready to work. He had been at the paper recycling plant for six years and was characterized as a very hard, dependable worker.

Psychological reports noted a delayed development from about four years of age and contained the labels "Middle grade imbecile," "TMR," and "educable to a very limited degree." Don was never institutionalized. He lived with his family on a farm before coming to the workshop. Don was considered by the staff members as capable of greater independent living conditions, and possibly, of living alone.

Max, a twenty-four year old male, was anoxic at birth and contracted encephalitis at the age of six. His mother was characterized in his personal files as a "disturbed and overprotective woman with paranoid features." Max's father died when he was a child. Max spent several years in a state hospital, to which he was returned halfway through the research period on account of behavioral problems.

Max obtained a high school diploma while in a state school. His psychological reports contained the label "EMR," "Schizophrenic personality of the chronic undifferentiated type," and "a schizophrenic boy who is retarded at the EMR level." IQ scores and subscores ranged from 76 to 98.

Work evaluations noted a concentrated attitude to work (sorting zippers). Within the structure of the group home setting he was difficult to manage. He often was uncooperative, or behaved "crazy," such as wandering around outside in the middle of the night. His talk was at times incoherent, at other times, very clear.

Max was on heavy medication for residual seizure disorders as well as on tranquilizers.

Appendix B

QUESTIONNAIRE TO HOUSEPARENTS — A VALIDITY PROCEDURE

Dear Houseparent:

As you are aware, I have carried out a research project over the past eight months, which involved many visits to the adult cottages, to recreation events, and participation in outings into the community.

The purpose of this research was to gain insight into ways by which the residents of the cottages made sense out of their daily living. This was done through participant observation, which involved interacting, reacting, asking questions, looking, and listening in an unobtrusive way, in order to obtain information that is typical of the residents' natural patterns of behavior.

It is now time to assess the validity of the data obtained from these research procedures; that is, to assess the extent to which I was able to make representative observations of the residents' behaviors. Your perspective is one aspect of this validity process. Therefore, I would much appreciate your cooperation by freely responding to the following questions:

1. Do you think that the residents' behavior during the participant observation visits was typical of their usual behavior? Did my presence and interaction with the residents or with the staff interfere, in any way, with the residents' usual behavior? Please, be specific.
2. From having observed my interaction with the residents, how would you describe the relationship that developed between us?
3. Did my presence, at any time, interfere with your involvement

as a staff member?

4. Is there any other aspect of this research that you could comment on, that may in any way have had an impact upon obtaining representative observations?

Thank you very much.

Responses

Houseparent A: Houseparent (weekdays) of the men's cottage during the first six months of the eight months observation period.

Houseparent B: Weekend houseparent of the men's cottage through the entire observation period.

Houseparent C: Houseparent (weekdays) of the women's cottage during seven months of the eight months observation period.

Houseparent D: Weekend houseparent of the men's cottage through the entire observation period.

Question 1. Do you think that the residents' behavior during the participant observation visits was typical of their usual behavior? Did my presence and interaction with the residents or with the staff interfere, in any way, with the residents' usual behavior? Please, be specific.

Houseparent A: Over the course of my observations I noticed a continual decrease in nontypical behaviors during your participant observation activities. Your data for the end of your study would probably be more valid than for the beginning.

Houseparent B: I feel that the behaviors exhibited, during your interactions with the clients, were quite typical of the way I have seen them behave with others who have interacted with them.

Houseparent C: For the most part, the clients behavior was the same. However, when any outside person comes in some of the clients will dwell on a subject (e.g., boyfriends, past family experiences) on which they would not normally concentrate. I think they feel like someone new would not be bored with these old topics like a houseparent who has heard them before.

Houseparent D: The longer your visit, the more natural the people in the cottage would become. They were generally on better behavior with you than the staff who actually lived with them, close friends, or family. There were occasions when you interacted with someone without knowing of previous happenings that might have influenced you differently in that interaction. In these instances the person you are talking to can use you because s/he knows you don't know what has recently transpired.

Question 2. From having observed my interaction with the residents, how would you describe the relationship that developed between us?

Houseparent A: The residents accepted your presence as an ordinary daily/weekly activity or occurrence. The fact that you are female influenced the (male) clients interactions with you to some extent.

Houseparent B: I do feel that the clients could and did use you differently than they would a staff member. There were some behaviors that I could not tolerate because of the group needs but you could on a one to one basis. I have tried to keep a group or family unit perspective in order to facilitate the acquisition of the skills needed to live in this type of environment. Because of this, the group would take preference over individual needs. You, I think, with the men, were able to give and take on individual basis and I feel that your rapport with the clients was well established.

Houseparent C: I believe the relationship that developed was that of a friendship with someone who was interested in them and what they had to say.

Houseparent D: You were a good consistent visiting friend, easily recognized when you came over to the cottage. You appeared to them with a genuine feeling of concern.

Question 3. Did my presence, at any time, interfere with your involvement as a staff member?

Houseparent A: No.

Houseparent B: At no time did your interactions interfere with my involvement as a staff member. The clients, not being at work, have their own lives to lead. Anything that they can do independently of me or any other staff member will only better their adjustment into a more normal existence in which interactions with other people is a major aspect.

Houseparent C: Only maybe once or twice did your involvement with the clients have an effect. It was in the form of a carry-over from conversation of boyfriend or family, which lead the client to dwell on the subject until she was upset. However, this only happened a couple of times.

Houseparent D: No. I strongly feel that your presence generally helped the atmosphere of the cottage and that you were welcome there by all.

Question 4. Is there any other aspect of this research that you could comment on, that may in any way have had an impact upon obtaining representative observations?

Houseparent A: Male and female roles are different in mixed groups. You probably did not get a totally representative sample of male clients in regards to sexually related discussions and/or activities.

Houseparent B: No response.

Houseparent C: I appreciated the fact that you as an observer came to me for explanations of various conversations. I feel that this helped give you a more valid observation.

Houseparent D: As an outsider looking in I would say that you saw a good representation of their daily lives. You treated them with the respect they all well deserved, not knowing or seemingly caring about some of the negative subtle behaviors involved in their interactions, known to the staff who work daily with these people. This is an important point in your favor in that you wanted to gather information directly from the clients.

REFERENCES

Abelson, R. B. and Johnson, R. C. Heterosexual and aggressive behaviors among institutionalized retardates. *Mental Retardation,* 1969, *7,* 28-31.

Becker, H. S. & Geer, B. Participant observation and interviewing: A comparison. In W. J. Filstead (Ed.), *Qualitative Methodology: Firsthand Involvement with the Social World.* Chicago: Markham Publishing Co., 1970.

Blatt, B. Public policy and the education of children with special needs. *Exceptional Children,* 1972, *38,* 537-548.

Blatt, B. Issues and values. In B. Blatt, D. Biklen & R. Bogdan (Eds.), *An Alternative Textbook in Special Education.* People, schools, and other institutions. Denver: Love Publishing, 1977.

Bogdan, R. B. & Taylor, S. A. *Introduction of Qualitative Research Methods.* New York: John Wiley, 1975.

Bogdan, R. B. & Taylor, S. A. The judged, not the judges: An insider's view of mental retardation. *American Psychologist,* 1976, *31* (1), 47-52.

Braginski, D. D. & Braginski, B. M. *Hansels and Gretels — Studies of Children in Institutions for the Mentally Retarded.* New York: Holt, Rinehart, & Winston, 1971.

Brantlinger, E. A. Effects of in-service training on attitudes of residential care staff about the sexual needs and rights of mentally retarded residents. Unpublished doctoral dissertation, Indiana University, 1978.

Brooks, P. H. & Baumeister, A. A. A plea for consideration of ecological validity in the experimental psychology of mental retardation: A guest editorial. *American Journal of Mental Deficiency,* 1977, *81* (5), 407-416.

Deisher, R. W. Sexual behavior of retarded in institutions. In F. F. de la Cruz & G. D. La Veck (Eds.), *Human Sexuality and the Mentally Retarded.* New York: Brunner/Mazel, 1973.

Dunn, L. M. Special education for the mildly retarded — Is much of it justifiable? *Exceptional Children,* 1968, *34,* 5-22.

Edgerton, R. B. *The Cloak of Competence: Stigma in the Lives of the Mentally Retarded.* Berkeley: University of California Press, 1967.

Edgerton, R. B. Mental retardation in non-Western societies: Toward a cross-cultural perspective on incompetence. In H. C. Haywood (Ed.), *Social-Cultural Aspects of Mental Retardation.* Proceedings of the Peabody NIHM Conference. New York: Meredith Corporation, 1970.

Edgerton, R. B. Some socio-cultural research considerations. In F. F. de la Cruz & G. D. La Veck (Eds.), *Human Sexuality and the Mentally Retarded.* New York: Brunner/Mazel, 1973.

Edgerton, R. B. Issues relating to the quality of life among mentally retarded persons. In M. J. Begab & S. A. Richardson (Eds.), *The Mentally Retarded and Society.* Baltimore: University Park Press, 1975.

Edgerton, R. B. & Bercovici, S. M. The cloak of competence — years later. *American Journal of Mental Deficiency,* 1976, *80* (5), 485-497.

Edgerton, R. B. & Sabagh, G. From mortification to aggrandizement: Changing self concepts in the careers of the mentally retarded. *Psychiatry,* 1962, *25,* 263-272.

Farber, B. *Mental Retardation.* Boston: Houghton Mifflin, 1968.

Garuth, D. G. Human sexuality in a halfway house. In F. F. de la Cruz & G. D. La Veck (Eds.), *Human Sexuality and the Mentally Retarded.* New York: Brunner/Mazel, 1973.

Gebhard, P. H. Sexual behavior of the mentally retarded. In F. F. de la Cruz & G. D. La Veck (Eds.), *Human Sexuality and the Mentally Retarded.* New York: Brunner/Mazel, 1973.

Glaser, B. G. & Strauss, A. L. *The Discovery of Grounded Theory: Strategies for Qualitative Research.* Chicago: Aldine Publication, 1967.

Gunzberg, H. *Social Competence and Mental Handicap.* Baltimore: The Williams and Wlkins Company, 1968.

Gordon, S. Missing in special education: Sex. *Journal of Special Education,* 1971, *5,* 351-354.

Gordon, S. A response to Warren Johnson. In F. F. de la Cruz & G. D. La Veck (Eds.), *Human Sexuality and the Mentally Retarded.* New York: Brunner/Mazel, 1973.

Gordon, S. Is parenting for everybody? *The Exceptional Parent,* 1977, *7,* 8-10.

Hall, E. T. *The Silent Language.* New York: Doubleday, 1959.

Hall, E. T. Mental health research and out-of-awareness cultural systems. In L. Nader & T. Maretzki (Eds.), *Cultural Illness and Health,* Washington, D.C.: American Anthropological Association, 1973.

Henshel, A. M. *The Forgotten Ones: A Sociological Study of Anglo and Chicano Retardates.* Austin, Texas: University of Texas Press, 1972.

Heshusius, L. Meaning in the lives of young adults labeled retarded in a group-home: A participant observation study. Unpublished doctoral dissertation, Indiana University, 1978.

Hilbert, R. A. Approaching reason's edge: "Nonsense" as the final solution to the problem of meaning. *Sociological Inquiry,* 1977, *47,* 25-31.

Hobbs, N. *The Futures of Children.* San Francisco: Jossey-Bass Publishing, 1975.

Johnson, W. R. Sex education of the mentally retarded. In F. F. de la Cruz & G. D. La Veck (Eds.), *Human Sexuality and the Mentally Re-*

tarded. New York: Brunner/Mazel, 1973.

Jones, R. L. Labels and stigma in special education. *Exceptional Children,* 1972, *38,* 553-564.

Lofland, J. Analyzing social settings. *A Guide to Qualitative Observation and Analysis.* Belmont, CA: Wadsworth Publishing Co., 1971.

MacMillan, D. L., Jones, R. L. & Aloia, G. F. The mentally retarded label: A theoretical analysis and review of research. *American Journal of Mental Deficiency,* 1974, *79* (3), 241-261.

van Manen, M. Linking ways of knowing with ways of being practical. *Curriculum Inquiry,* 1977, *6,* 205-229.

Mattinson, J. Marriage and mental handicap. In F. F. de la Cruz & G. D. La Veck (Eds.), *Human Sexuality and the Mentally Retarded.* New York: Brunner/Mazel, 1973.

Mattinson, J. *Marriage and Mental Handicap.* University of Pittsburgh Press, 1970.

Meyers, R. A couple that could. *Psychology Today,* 1978, *12* (6), 99-108.

Money, J. W. Keynote address — some thoughts on sexual taboos and the rights of the retarded. In F. F. de la Cruz & G. D. La Veck (Eds.), *Human Sexuality and the Mentally Retarded.* New York: Brunner/Mazel, 1973.

Morgenstern, M. Community attitudes toward sexuality of the retarded. In F. F. de la Cruz & G. D. La Veck (Eds.), *Human Sexuality and the Mentally Retarded.* New York: Brunner/Mazel, 1973.

Rhodes, W. C. *A Study of Child Variance.* Vol. 5 Conference Proceedings. Ann Arbor, Mich.: Institute for the study of mental retardation and related disabilities, University of Mich., 1975.

Smith, M. B. Perspectives of selfhood. *American Psychologist,* 1978, *33,* 1053-1063.

Taylor, S. & Bogdan, R. A phenomenological approach to "mental retardation." In B. Blatt, D. Biklen, & R. Bogdan (Eds.) *An Alternative Textbook in Special Education.* People, schools, and other institutions. Denver: Love Publishing, 1977.

Willems, E. P. Planning a rationale for naturalistic research. In E. P. Willems & H. L. Raush (Eds.), *Naturalistic Viewpoints in Psychological Research.* New York: Holt, Rinehart and Winston, 1969.

Willems, E. P. & Raush, H. L. (Eds.) *Naturalistic Viewpoints in Psychological Research.* New York: Holt, Rinehart and Winston, 1969.

Wilson, S. The use of ethnographic techniques in educational research. *Review of Educational Research,* 1977, *47* (2), 245-265.

Wolfensberger, W. *Normalization.* The principle of normalization in human services. Toronto: National Institute on Mental Retardation, 1972.

Wolfensberger, W. Normalizing activation for the profoundly retarded and/or multiple handicapped. In B. Blatt, D. Biklen, & R. Bogdan (Eds.), *An Alternative Textbook in Special Education.* People, schools, and other institutions. Denver: Love Publishing, 1977.

INDEX

Q

R

S

T

V

W

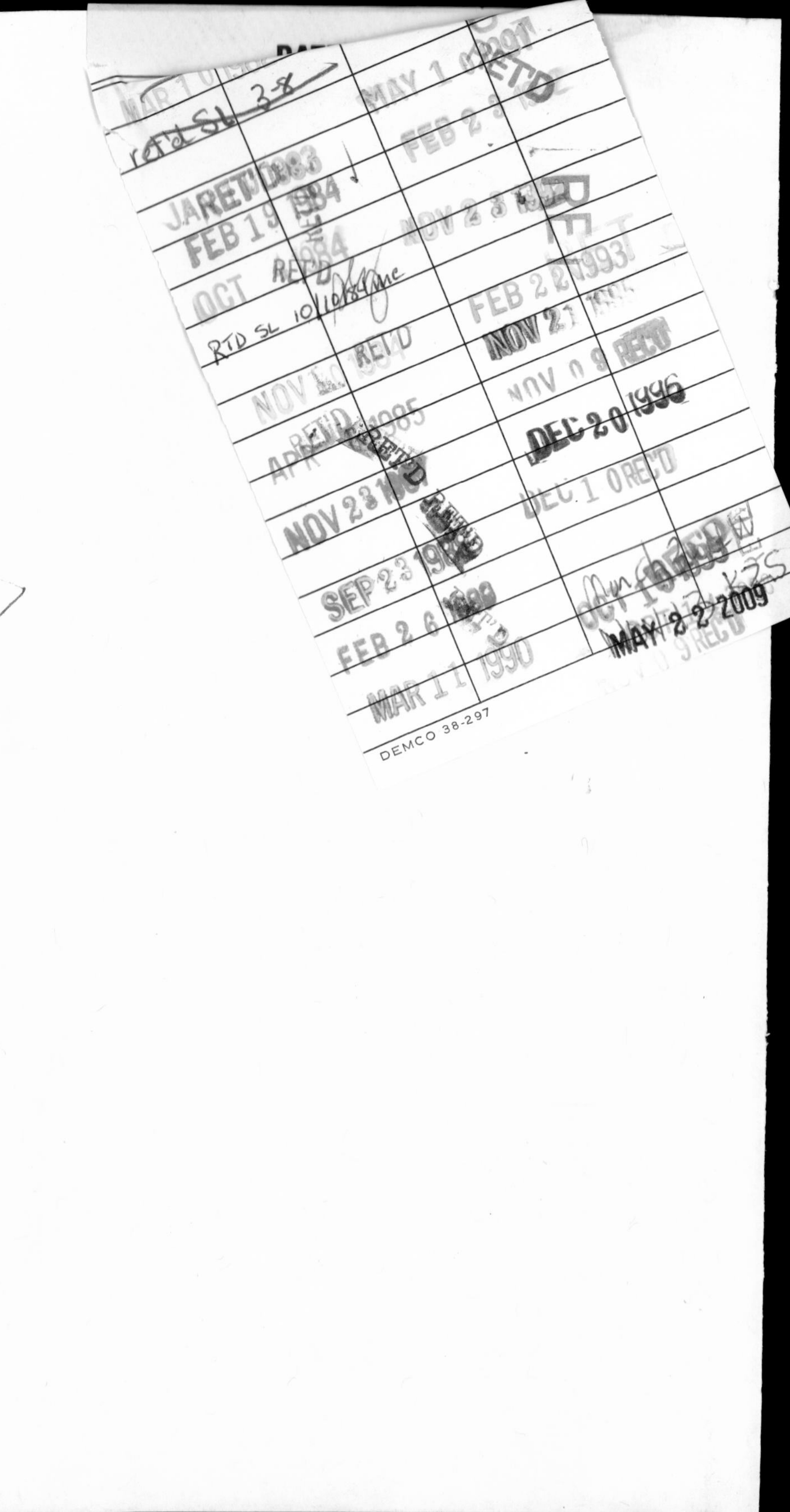